The art of

WINNING INTERVIEWS

-It's as simple as enjoying a cup of coffee-

Dr.Y. Narasimha Raja

Ph.D., MBA, M.Sc. Psychology
Asst. Professor –School of Management,
Presidency University, Bengaluru

Mob: +(91)8073205840
Email: ynraja.phd@gmail.com
Web: www.ynraja.com

The author articulated this book, with his research, various sources of books, electronic media, Social media, magazines, anecdotes, stories, journals, Interviewing with various experts, other speakers, and seminar participants. Primary and Secondary data have been considered. If any resemblance regarding the topic is purely coincidence as many examples and subject details have been collected from various sources. Regrettably, sources were not always renowned or available; hence, it became impractical to provide an accurate recognition.

MRP: Indian Rupees (INR) 300/-
Publishers: Notion Press
800, West El Camino Real #180,California USA 94040
Email : publish@notionpress.com
web: www.notionpress.com

Index

Preface

Lucky means, who gets the opportunity. Brilliant means , who creat the Opportunity, WINNER means, who uses the Opportunity.

This book, "The Art of Winning Interviews," is designed to equip you with the knowledge and strategies necessary to excel in interviews. It is structured into three critical stages:

Stage 1: Before the Interview In this stage, you will learn the essential techniques for crafting an impeccable resume, grooming yourself appropriately, managing interview stress, reflecting on past interview experiences, and understanding the fundamental manners expected from an applicant. Mastering these preparatory steps lays a solid foundation for a successful interview.

Stage 2: During the Interview This stage delves into the crucial moments of the interview itself. You will discover the do's and don'ts of interviews, and navigate through **meticulously** curated interview questions and answers. These questions span various categories such as personal, educational, organizational, experiential, behavioral, teamwork, dependability, decision-making, leadership, problem-solving, research, creativity, and integrity. Additionally, this stage addresses how to handle interviews that aren't going as planned, ensuring you remain composed and focused throughout.

Stage 3: After the Interview The final stage focuses on the post-interview phase, including strategies for salary negotiation, understanding reasons for not receiving offers, and effective follow-up techniques. These insights will help you maintain a professional demeanor and leave a lasting impression on potential employers.

With you and for you

Dr Y Narasimha Raja

About Author Dr Y Narasimha Raja

f

Dr Y Narasimha Raja multifaceted professional with significant contributions to the fields of Psychology, Management, and Human Resources His extensive educational background, with a PhD in Management Studies, and Master of Business Administration, Master of Science in Psychology and multiple master's degrees, complements his over 19 years of experience in corporate and academic sectors across India and internationally As an award-winning HR practitioner and corporate trainer, Dr Raja's expertise has been recognized by numerous prestigious awards

Book Publications

1. Highly Effective Parenting Skills
2. Highly Effective Teaching Skills
3. The best & smart Teaching techniques
4. Happy Parenting Skills
5. Stage Fear
6. Highly effective Public Speaking Skills
7. Phobias-Overview on 165 phobias
8. Neuro Disorders
9. Counseling Skills
10. How to change life better?
11. Positive Psychology for a Successful people
12. Don't Overthink
13. The art of Winning Interviews

Stage1

BEFORE INTERVIEW

Chapter-1
Mastering Resume Writing Techniques

Your resume is often the first impression you make on potential employers It serves as your personal marketing document, showcasing your skills, experiences, and qualifications Crafting a compelling resume is crucial to standing out in a competitive job market This chapter will guide you through effective resume writing techniques, helping you create a document that not only grabs attention but also lands interviews

Purpose of a Resume: The primary purpose of a resume is to secure an interview by presenting your qualifications in a clear, concise, and compelling manner It should highlight your professional history, skills, achievements, and educational background

Types of Resumes

There are several types of resumes, each suited for different career stages and situations:

1. **Chronological Resume**: Focuses on your work history, listing positions in reverse chronological order Ideal for individuals with a consistent work history

2. **Functional Resume**: Emphasizes skills and experiences rather than chronological work history Suitable for career changers or those with gaps in employment

3. **Combination Resume**: Merges elements of both chronological and functional resumes, highlighting skills while providing a chronological work history.

Structuring Your Resume

Contact Information : Include your full name, phone number, email address, and LinkedIn profile Ensure your email address is professional

Professional Summary : A professional summary is a brief statement at the top of your resume that highlights your most relevant qualifications and career goals It should be tailored to the specific job you're applying for

Example: *"Experienced marketing professional with over five years of experience in digital marketing, content creation, and social media management Proven track record of driving engagement and increasing brand awareness Seeking to leverage expertise in a dynamic marketing role at XYZ Company"*

Work Experience : List your work experience in reverse chronological order, starting with your most recent job For each position, include:

- Job title
- Company name
- Location (city, state)
- Dates of employment
- Bullet points outlining your responsibilities and achievements

Common Mistakes to Avoid

1. **Spelling and Grammar Errors**: Typos, misspellings, and grammatical mistakes can make a poor first impression Proofread multiple times or use a grammar checking tool to avoid these errors

2. **Unprofessional Email Address**: Using an unprofessional email address can seem unprofessional Always use a simple, professional email address for job applications

3. **Lack of Focus or Objective**: Failing to include a clear objective or summary statement can leave recruiters unsure about your career goals Tailor this section to the specific job you are applying for

4. **Too Long or Too Short**:: Resumes that are too long (more than two pages) or too short (less than one page) can be ineffective Aim for a concise, one- to two-page resume that highlights relevant information.

5. **Irrelevant Information:** Including unrelated work experiences or personal information (like age, marital status, or unrelated hobbies) can clutter your resume Focus on relevant job experience and skills

6. **Poor Formatting:** Inconsistent fonts, sizes, and spacing can make your resume difficult to read Use a clean, professional format with consistent headings and bullet points

7. **Using Vague Language:** Using vague terms like "responsible for" without specifics can be uninformative Use action verbs and quantify achievements to demonstrate your impact (eg, "Increased sales by 20% in six months")

8. **Not Tailoring the Resume:** Sending the same resume for every job application can reduce your chances Customize your resume for each job by highlighting relevant skills and xperiences

9. **Leaving Out Keywords:** Many companies use Applicant Tracking Systems (ATS) to screen resumes Not including relevant keywords from the job description can lead to your resume being overlooked

10. **Lack of Contact Information:** Failing to include up-to-date contact information can make it impossible for employers to reach you Ensure your phone number, email address, and LinkedIn profile (if applicable) are current and visible

Chapter-2
Grooming for Interview

First impressions are pivotal, especially in the context of job interviews Grooming goes beyond mere physical appearance; it encompasses a comprehensive preparation strategy that includes attire, body language, communication skills, and overall professionalism This chapter delves into effective grooming techniques for interviews, providing practical insights to help candidates present themselves as the best fit for the role

1. Understanding the Importance of Grooming

Grooming is essential because it reflects one's attention to detail, self-discipline, and respect for the interview process A well-groomed appearance can significantly influence the interviewer's perception of a candidate's suitability for the job It's about showcasing the best version of oneself, projecting confidence, and demonstrating a serious attitude toward the opportunity

2. Dress Code: Dressing for Success

- **Research the Company Culture** Understanding the company's culture helps in selecting the appropriate attire For instance, a corporate firm may require formal business wear, while a tech startup might have a more casual dress code Researching beforehand ensures alignment with company expectations

- **Choosing the Right Outfit :** For men, a well-fitted suit, a crisp dress shirt, and a conservative tie are usually safe bets Women might opt for a tailored dress, a skirt suit, or slacks with a blouse Neutral colors like black, navy, and grey are preferred as they exude professionalism

- **Attention to Detail :** Ensure that clothes are clean, ironed, and free of any stains or wrinkles Shoes should be polished and in good condition Accessories should be minimal and not distracting Overall, the goal is to appear polished and put-together

3. **Personal Hygiene and Grooming**

a) **Hair and Makeup :** Hair should be clean, neatly styled, and professional-looking For men, facial hair should be trimmed or shaved cleanly Women should opt for natural makeup that enhances features without being overpowering

b) **Skin Care :** A fresh, clean face is crucial Ensure your skin is well-moisturized, and avoid heavy fragrances that might be distracting Good oral hygiene is also essential; make sure your breath is fresh and teeth are clean

c) **Nail Care:**Keep nails clean and trimmed For women, if you choose to wear nail polish, opt for neutral colors that don't draw excessive attention

4. **Body Language: Non-Verbal Communication**

a) **Posture :** Maintain an upright posture, which conveys confidence and attentiveness Slouching can be perceived as disinterest or lack of confidence

b) **Eye Contact :** Make regular eye contact to show engagement and sincerity Avoid staring, which can be uncomfortable, but frequent eye contact indicates confidence and interest

c) **Handshake :** A firm handshake is a universal sign of confidence Ensure your hand is dry and firm without being overly strong Practice with friends if needed to get it just right

d) **Gestures :** Use hand gestures moderately to emphasize points, but avoid excessive movements that can be distracting Keep your hands visible and relaxed, not fidgeting or crossing arms

5. **Communication Skills: Articulate and Confident**

a) **Clear and Concise Speech :** Speak clearly and at a moderate pace Avoid using filler words like "um" or "like" excessively Practice your answers to common interview questions to improve fluency and confidence

b) **Active Listening :** Show that you are engaged by nodding and making affirming sounds at appropriate times Reflect on what the interviewer says before responding, demonstrating that you are attentive and thoughtful

c) **Professional Tone :** Maintain a professional tone throughout the interview Be polite and respectful, avoiding slang or overly casual language Adapt your language to mirror the formality of the interview setting

6 Preparation: The Foundation of Confidence

a) **Research :** Thoroughly research the company, its culture, the role you are applying for, and industry trends This knowledge will help you tailor your answers and demonstrate genuine interest

b) **Mock Interviews :** Practice with friends, family, or career services Mock interviews can help identify areas for improvement and increase your comfort level

c) **Questions to Ask :** Prepare insightful questions to ask the interviewer This demonstrates your enthusiasm for the role and helps you gather information to assess if the company is the right fit for you

7 Mental and Emotional Preparation

a) **Visualization :** Visualize the interview process, from walking in to answering questions confidently This mental rehearsal can reduce anxiety and improve performance

b) **Stress Management :** Practice relaxation techniques such as deep breathing or meditation Staying calm and composed is crucial for effective communication and decision-making

c) **Positive Mindset :** Maintain a positive mindset Confidence can be a self-fulfilling prophecy; if you believe in your ability to succeed, you are more likely to perform well

Remember, the goal is to create a positive and lasting impression that convinces the interviewer of your suitability for the role

Chapter:3
Handling Stress During Interviews

Interviews are inherently stressful experiences, often determining the course of one's career Handling stress effectively during an interview can significantly improve performance, allowing candidates to showcase their true potential This chapter provides comprehensive strategies for managing stress before, during, and after an interview, ensuring candidates can present their best selves confidently and competently

Understanding Interview Stress :

Interview stress arises from the pressure to perform well, the fear of the unknown, and the desire to make a positive impression It can manifest physically through symptoms such as sweating, shaking, or a rapid heartbeat, and mentally through anxiety, forgetfulness, or negative thoughts Recognizing these symptoms is the first step toward managing them effectively

1. Pre-Interview Preparation

a) **Research and Knowledge :** Thorough preparation can significantly reduce anxiety Research the company's history, values, culture, and recent developments Understand the job description and the skills required This knowledge not only boosts confidence but also helps tailor responses to align with the company's expectations

b) **Practice and Rehearsal :** Practice answering common interview questions with friends, family, or mentors Mock interviews can simulate the actual experience, reducing unfamiliarity and anxiety Recording these sessions can help identify areas for improvement

c) **Plan Your Journey :** Ensure you know the interview location and the best route to get there Plan to arrive at least 15 minutes early to account for any unforeseen delays Knowing you have ample time to reach the venue can alleviate stress related to punctuality.

d) **Prepare Your Outfit :** Choose an appropriate outfit the day before the interview Ensure it is clean, ironed, and fits well Dressing professionally can boost self-confidence and help make a positive first impression

e) **Organize Your Documents :** Prepare a folder with multiple copies of your resume, a list of references, and any other necessary documents Having everything organized and ready can reduce last-minute stress

2. Mental and Emotional Preparation

a) **Positive Visualization :** Visualize a successful interview Imagine walking in confidently, answering questions effectively, and receiving positive feedback This mental rehearsal can reduce anxiety and build self-assurance

b) **Stress-Relief Techniques :** Practice relaxation techniques such as deep breathing, progressive muscle relaxation, or meditation These can help calm the mind and reduce physical symptoms of stress

c) **Affirmations and Positive Self-Talk :** Use positive affirmations to reinforce confidence Phrases like "I am prepared and capable" can replace negative thoughts with empowering ones Self-compassion and positive self-talk are crucial in maintaining a positive mindset

d) **Healthy Lifestyle Choices :** Maintain a healthy lifestyle leading up to the interview Get adequate sleep, eat nutritious meals, and exercise regularly These habits contribute to overall well-being and resilience to stress

3. During the Interview

a) **Manage Physical Symptoms:** If you feel nervous, take a few deep breaths to calm your heart rate Sit up straight, maintain eye contact, and use open body language These physical cues can help you feel more in control

b) **Active Listening:** Focus on the interviewer's questions without anticipating what to say next Active listening not only helps you understand the question better but also demonstrates engagement and respect.

c) **Structured Responses:** Use the STAR (Situation, Task, Action, Result) method to structure your responses This technique helps you provide clear, concise, and relevant answers, reducing the likelihood of rambling due to nervousness

d) **Pause and Think**It's okay to take a moment to think before answering a question Pausing shows that you are thoughtful and considerate in your responses It also gives you time to compose yourself and reduce anxiety

e) **Stay Present:** Focus on the current moment rather than worrying about the next question or dwelling on a previous answer Staying present helps maintain composure and improves overall performance.

f) **Positive Body Language:** Smile, nod, and use appropriate hand gestures to convey confidence and enthusiasm Positive body language can create a favorable impression and help you feel more at ease.

4. Cognitive Techniques

a) **Cognitive Restructuring :** Challenge negative thoughts and replace them with positive, realistic ones Instead of thinking, "I'm going to mess up," reframe it to, "I've prepared well, and I will do my best"
b) **Mindfulness :** Practice mindfulness to stay focused on the present moment Techniques such as mindful breathing or body scans can help manage anxiety and keep you grounded during the interview
c) **Anchoring :** Use an "anchor" to maintain calmness, such as a subtle touch to a piece of jewelry or a pressure point This physical cue can help center your mind and reduce stress.

5. Post-Interview Strategies

a) Reflect on the Experience : After the interview, take some time to reflect on what went well and areas for improvement This reflection should be constructive, focusing on learning and growth rather than self-criticism

b) Stress-Relief Activities : Engage in activities that help you unwind, such as exercise, hobbies, or spending time with loved ones These activities can help dissipate residual stress and promote relaxation

c) **Follow-Up :** Send a thank-you email to the interviewer expressing appreciation for the opportunity This not only demonstrates professionalism but also provides closure to the interview process.

6. Long-Term Stress Management

a) **Continuous Learning :** Keep enhancing your skills and knowledge through continuous learning This not only makes you more competitive but also boosts self-confidence and reduces anxiety about future interviews.

b) **Build a Support System :** Surround yourself with supportive friends, family, and mentors who can provide encouragement and constructive feedback A strong support system can help you navigate the stresses of job searching and interviewing.

c) **Develop Resilience :** Cultivate resilience by facing challenges and learning from setbacks Building resilience helps you bounce back from failures and maintain a positive outlook.

d) **Professional Help :** If interview stress becomes overwhelming, consider seeking professional help from a therapist.

Chapter-4
Recollect the earlier Interview Failures

Interviews can be daunting, and many factors can contribute to their success or failure Understanding common reasons for interview failures can help candidates better prepare and avoid these pitfalls Below are some key reasons why interviews might not go as planned:

1. Lack of Preparation

Insufficient Company Research : Failing to research the company's history, values, culture, and recent developments can lead to unprepared and irrelevant responses, indicating a lack of genuine interest Interviewers often ask questions to gauge your understanding of their organization When you can't provide specific insights or connect your answers to the company's objectives and challenges, it suggests a lack of diligence and enthusiasm Effective preparation involves studying the company's website, recent news articles, and social media channels, as well as understanding its position in the industry

Unfamiliarity with the Job Role: Not thoroughly understanding the job description and the required skills can result in answers that do not align with the job's expectations, making it seem like you are not a gfood fit It's crucial to dissect the job posting, identify the key responsibilities and required skills, and prepare examples from your experience that demonstrate your ability to fulfill these requirements Understanding the job role helps in articulating how your background, skills, and career aspirations align with the position

Poor Practice: Lack of practice can lead to stumbling over answers, nervousness, and an inability to effectively communicate your qualifications and experiences Practicing common interview questions, especially those relevant to your industry, can significantly boost your confidence Mock interviews with friends, mentors, or career counselors can simulate the interview environment, helping you become more comfortable and articulate Recording your practice sessions can provide valuable feedback on areas needing improvementf

2. Inadequate Responses

Vague Answers : Providing vague or general answers instead of specific examples can make it hard for the interviewer to gauge your actual experience and skills Employers look for candidates who can demonstrate their competencies with concrete examples Using the STAR (Situation, Task, Action, Result) method helps structure your answers, making them more compelling and relevant

Inability to Quantify Achievements : Failing to use numbers and specific details to highlight your achievements can result in a less impactful impression of your capabilities Quantifying your accomplishments, such as "increased sales by 20%" or "managed a team of 10," provides a clear picture of your effectiveness and contributions This specificity can set you apart from other candidates who provide more generic responses

Overly Long or Rambling Responses : Long-winded answers can dilute your message and make it harder for interviewers to remember key points about your qualifications Being concise and to the point ensures that your answers remain focused and relevant Practicing concise responses helps in maintaining the interviewer's interest and keeping the conversation dynamic

3. Poor Body Language

Lack of Eye Contact: Avoiding eye contact can be perceived as a lack of confidence or honesty Maintaining appropriate eye contact shows that you are engaged, trustworthy, and confident It's important to balance eye contact so it feels natural, avoiding staring which can be uncomfortable

Negative Posture: Slouching, crossed arms, or fidgeting can indicate nervousness, discomfort, or disinterest Positive body language, such as sitting upright, leaning slightly forward, and keeping your hands visible, demonstrates attentiveness and confidence Controlling your posture helps in projecting a professional image

Weak Handshake: A weak handshake can be interpreted as a lack of confidence and professionalism A firm, but not overpowering, handshake is a universal gesture of confidence and respect It sets the tone for the interview, making a strong first impression

4. Negative Attitude

Criticizing Past Employers : Speaking negatively about past employers or colleagues can reflect poorly on your attitude and suggest potential future issues It's important to remain professional and diplomatic, focusing on what you learned from past experiences rather than dwelling on negatives This approach shows maturity and a positive outlook

Overconfidence or Arrogance : Overconfidence or appearing arrogant can be off-putting and may suggest an inability to work well in a team or accept feedback Confidence is essential, but it should be balanced with humility and a willingness to learn Demonstrating respect for the interviewer and the opportunity can help avoid the perception of arrogance.

Lack of Enthusiasm : A lack of enthusiasm can make it seem like you are not genuinely interested in the role or the company Showing enthusiasm through your tone of voice, body language, and questions can convey your genuine interest and excitement about the opportunity Employers are more likely to hire candidates who seem passionate and motivated

5. Inability to Handle Stress

Visible Nervousness: Excessive nervousness can impact your ability to think clearly and communicate effectively, leading to poor performance Techniques such as deep breathing, visualization, and positive self-talk can help manage interview anxiety Staying calm and composed allows you to present your best self

Poor Response to Difficult Questions : Inability to handle challenging questions calmly and thoughtfully can indicate a lack of problem-solving skills and resilience Preparing for tough questions and practicing calm, structured responses can help It's okay to take a moment to think before answering, showing that you are thoughtful and composed under pressure

6. Misalignment with Company Culture

Incompatible Values : If your personal values and working style do not align with the company's culture, it may become evident during the interview, affecting your chances Understanding the company's culture through research and reflecting on your own values can help assess compatibility Demonstrating how your values align with the company's can strengthen your candidacy

Failure to Demonstrate Cultural Fit : Not demonstrating an understanding or appreciation of the company's culture and values can lead to concerns about your potential integration into the team Sharing examples of how you have thrived in similar environments and articulating why you are excited about the company's culture can mitigate these concerns

7. Lack of Soft Skills

Poor Communication Skills : Ineffective communication can hinder your ability to clearly convey your qualifications and experiences Good communication involves clear articulation, active listening, and appropriate body language Practicing these skills can improve your interview performance

Lack of Teamwork or Collaboration Skills : Not providing examples of teamwork and collaboration can suggest that you may struggle in a team-oriented environment Employers value candidates who can work well with others, so it's important to highlight experiences where you successfully collaborated and contributed to a team's success

Ineffective Problem-Solving Skills : Inability to provide examples of problem-solving skills can indicate a lack of critical thinking and adaptability Sharing specific instances where you identified a problem, developed a solution, and implemented it successfully can demonstrate your problem-solving abilities

8. Inappropriate Attire

Overly Casual Dress : Dressing too casually can suggest a lack of respect for the interview process and the company's professionalism Understanding the company's dress code and erring on the side of formality can ensure you make a positive impression Professional attire shows that you take the opportunity seriously

Inappropriate or Distracting Clothing : Wearing clothing that is too flashy or inappropriate can distract from your qualifications and make a negative impression Choosing conservative and professional attire helps keep the focus on your skills and experience It's important to avoid clothing that might be considered unprofessional or distracting.

9. Poor Follow-Up

Lack of a Thank-You Note : Failing to send a thank-you note after the interview can suggest a lack of appreciation and professionalism A well-crafted thank-you note shows gratitude, reinforces your interest in the role, and provides an opportunity to reiterate your qualifications

Poorly Written Follow-Up : A thank-you note with typos or generic content can reflect poorly on your attention to detail and genuine interest Taking the time to personalize the note and proofread it carefully demonstrates professionalism.

10. **Unrealistic Expectations & Overemphais on salary**

Focusing too much on salary and benefits rather than the role and the company can suggest that you are more interested in compensation than the job itself .

Chapter-5
Interview manners from the applicant side.

Navigating the interview process with the right manners and etiquette can significantly impact your chances of success This chapter delves into the essential manners and behaviors that applicants should exhibit to make a positive and lasting impression on their potential employers By adhering to these guidelines, candidates can present themselves as professional, respectful, and well-prepared

1. Punctuality

Importance of Arriving on Time : Arriving on time for an interview demonstrates respect for the interviewer's schedule and shows that you are organized and reliable Being late can create a negative first impression and suggest a lack of commitment or time management skills Timeliness reflects your overall professionalism and reliability, essential traits employers seek in candidates It shows that you value the interviewer's time and are serious about the opportunity

Plan Your Route : Plan your journey in advance to ensure you account for any potential delays Check traffic conditions, public transportation schedules, and parking availability Aim to arrive at least 10-15 minutes early to allow time for any unforeseen circumstances This extra time acts as a buffer against unexpected delays, reducing stress and allowing you to start the interview in a calm and collected manner

Communicate Delays : If you encounter an unavoidable delay, contact the interviewer as soon as possible to inform them of your situation and provide an estimated arrival time Apologize for the inconvenience and demonstrate your consideration for their time Effective communication shows that you are responsible and considerate, qualities that reflect well on your candidacy

2. Dress Appropriately

Understanding Dress Codes : Different companies have different dress codes, ranging from formal business attire to business casual Research the company culture to determine the appropriate level of formality for your interview attire Dressing in line with the company's standards shows that you have done your homework and respect their norms.

Professional and Conservative Choices : Opt for professional, conservative clothing that fits well and is clean and wrinkle-free Avoid overly casual, flashy, or distracting outfits When in doubt, err on the side of formality A well-chosen outfit can boost your confidence and ensure that your appearance reflects your professionalism and seriousness about the role

Grooming and Hygiene : Ensure that you are well-groomed, with clean hair, nails, and minimal use of perfumes or colognes Pay attention to details such as polished shoes and tidy accessories, as these can contribute to a polished appearance Good grooming shows attention to detail and respect for the interview process

3. Body Language

Confident Posture : Maintain a confident and open posture by sitting up straight, keeping your shoulders back, and avoiding slouching This body language conveys confidence, attentiveness, and respect Your posture can significantly influence the interviewer's perception of your confidence and engagement

Eye Contact : Make appropriate eye contact with the interviewer to show that you are engaged and interested in the conversation Avoid staring, which can be uncomfortable, but maintain steady eye contact to build rapport Good eye contact indicates sincerity and helps establish a connection with the interviewer

Positive Gestures : Use positive gestures such as nodding and smiling to indicate that you are attentive and receptive Avoid crossing your arms, fidgeting, or making excessive hand movements, as these can be distracting or convey nervousness Positive gestures enhance your verbal communication and demonstrate your enthusiasm and openness

4. Communication Skills

Clear and Concise Responses : Provide clear and concise answers to interview questions Avoid rambling or going off-topic, and use the STAR (Situation, Task, Action, Result) method to structure your responses effectively Clear communication ensures that your key points are understood and highlights your ability to convey information succinctly

Active Listening : Practice active listening by nodding, maintaining eye contact, and occasionally summarizing or reflecting back what the interviewer has said This shows that you are fully engaged and understand the conversation Active listening builds rapport and demonstrates that you value the interviewer's input

Politeness and Respect : Use polite language and address the interviewer with appropriate titles and names Avoid interrupting, and wait for the interviewer to finish speaking before responding Show respect by acknowledging their questions and insights thoughtfully Politeness and respect foster a positive interaction and leave a good impression

5. Professionalism

Turn Off Mobile Devices : Ensure that your mobile phone and other electronic devices are turned off or set to silent mode before the interview begins This prevents interruptions and shows that you are fully focused on the interview Professionalism in this aspect demonstrates your commitment and consideration for the interview process

Bring Necessary Documents : Bring multiple copies of your resume, a list of references, and any other required documents in a neat folder or portfolio This demonstrates that you are prepared and organized Having the necessary documents readily available shows foresight and readiness, reinforcing your professionalism

Avoid Negative Talk : Refrain from speaking negatively about past employers, colleagues, or experiences Focus on positive aspects and what you have learned from your past roles This shows maturity and a positive attitude Maintaining a positive tone reflects well on your character and professional demeanor

6. Asking Questions

Prepare Thoughtful Questions : Prepare a list of thoughtful questions to ask the interviewer about the role, company culture, and career development opportunities This shows your genuine interest in the position and helps you gather valuable information Thoughtful questions demonstrate that you are proactive and engaged

Show Enthusiasm : Ask questions that reflect your enthusiasm for the role and the company Inquire about team dynamics, company goals, and how your skills can contribute to the organization's success Enthusiastic questions indicate that you are passionate about the opportunity and keen to contribute

Avoid Self-Centered Questions : Avoid questions that focus solely on what the company can do for you, such as salary, benefits, or vacation time Instead, balance these with questions that demonstrate your interest in contributing to the company's goals This approach shows that you are aligned with the company's vision and priorities

7. Follow-Up

Send a Thank-You Note : Send a thank-you note or email within 24 hours of the interview Express your appreciation for the opportunity, reiterate your interest in the position, and mention a specific topic or insight from the interview that resonated with you A timely thank-you note reinforces your interest and professionalism

Personalize Your Message : Personalize your thank-you message to each interviewer, highlighting individual discussions or connections This shows your attentiveness and leaves a positive impression Personalized follow-ups demonstrate that you value each interviewer's time and input

Proofread Carefully : Ensure that your thank-you note is free of typos and grammatical errors A well-written and polished message reflects your attention to detail and professionalism Careful proofreading ensures that your follow-up communication is clear and professional

8. Handling Difficult Questions

Stay Calm and Composed : If faced with a difficult question, take a moment to gather your thoughts before responding Staying calm and composed demonstrates your ability to handle pressure and think critically Composure under pressure highlights your problem-solving abilities and emotional intelligence

Be Honest and Transparent: Provide honest and transparent answers, even if the question addresses a challenging aspect of your background Authenticity is valued by employers, and honesty can build trust Transparency fosters trust and showcases your integrity

Stage2
DURING INTERVIEW

Chapter.6 - Do's & Don't's during Interview

Chapter.7- Interview Question & Answers

- About you
- Education Based Questions
- Organization based questions
- Experience based questions
- Behavioral based questions
- Teamwork based questions
- Dependable or Reliable questions
- Decision making Questions
- Leadership questions
- Problem solving questions
- Research Questions
- Creativity Questions
- Integrity Questions

Chapter.8 Handling challenges when an Interview is NOT Going Well

Chapter-6
Do's and Don't during Interview

Navigating an interview successfully requires more than just answering questions correctly; it involves demonstrating the right behaviors and avoiding common pitfalls This chapter provides a comprehensive guide on the dos and don'ts during an interview, offering detailed explanations for each point to help you make a positive and lasting impression

Dos During an Interview

Do Prepare Thoroughly : Preparation is key to success in any interview Research the company's history, values, products or services, and recent developments Understand the job role, its responsibilities, and the required skills This preparation allows you to tailor your responses to align with the company's needs and demonstrate your genuine interest in the position

- ✓ **Research the Company:** Know the company's mission, vision, and values Familiarize yourself with its products, services, market position, and competitors

- ✓ **Understand the Job Description:** Identify the key responsibilities and required skills Prepare examples from your experience that match these requirements

- ✓ **Practice Common Questions:** Anticipate common interview questions and practice your responses Use the STAR (Situation, Task, Action, Result) method to structure your answers effectively

Do Dress Appropriately : Your attire should reflect the company's dress code and the formality of the interview Dressing appropriately shows respect for the interviewer and the interview process

- ✓ **Match the Company Culture:** Research the company's dress code If unsure, opt for business professional attire
- ✓ **Choose Professional Attire:** Wear clean, well-fitted, and wrinkle-free clothes Avoid overly casual, flashy, or distracting outfits
- ✓ **Grooming and Hygiene:** Ensure you are well-groomed with clean hair and nails Minimize the use of perfumes or colognes

Do Arrive on Time: Punctuality is crucial Arriving on time shows that you are reliable, organized, and respectful of the interviewer's time

- ✓ **Plan Ahead:** Plan your route, account for potential delays, and aim to arrive 10-15 minutes early
- ✓ **Communicate Delays:** If you encounter unexpected delays, inform the interviewer as soon as possible and provide an estimated arrival time

Do Maintain Positive Body Language: Your body language communicates your confidence, interest, and professionalism

- ✓ **Confident Posture:** Sit up straight with your shoulders back Avoid slouching or crossing your arms
- ✓ **Eye Contact:** Maintain appropriate eye contact to show engagement and build rapport
- ✓ **Positive Gestures:** Use nodding and smiling to indicate attentiveness and receptiveness

Do Communicate Clearly and Concisely : Effective communication is essential to convey your qualifications and fit for the role

- ✓ **Clear Responses:** Provide clear and concise answers Avoid rambling or going off-topic
- ✓ **Active Listening:** Show that you are listening by nodding, maintaining eye contact, and summarizing key points
- ✓ **Polite Language:** Use respectful and professional language Address the interviewer by their title and name

Do Ask Thoughtful Questions: Asking questions shows your interest in the role and the company

- ✓ **Prepare Questions:** Prepare a list of thoughtful questions about the role, team, and company culture
- ✓ **Show Enthusiasm:** Ask questions that reflect your enthusiasm and desire to contribute
- ✓ **Balance Questions:** Avoid focusing solely on salary and benefits Balance these with questions about the company's goals and values

Don'ts During an Interview

Don't Be Late : Being late for an interview creates a negative first impression and suggests a lack of reliability and time management skills

- **Avoid Poor Planning:** Plan your journey and account for potential delays Aim to arrive early
- **Communicate Unavoidable Delays:** If you are unavoidably delayed, contact the interviewer immediately and apologize for the inconvenience

Don't Dress Inappropriately : Inappropriate attire can distract from your qualifications and show a lack of understanding of the company's culture

- **Avoid Overly Casual or Flashy Clothing:** Stick to professional and conservative attire that fits the company's dress code
- **Ensure Good Grooming:** Pay attention to grooming and hygiene Avoid strong perfumes or colognes

Don't Display Negative Body Language : Negative body language can undermine your verbal responses and create a poor impression

- **Avoid Poor Posture:** Don't slouch, cross your arms, or fidget These can convey nervousness or disinterest
- **Maintain Appropriate Eye Contact:** Avoid looking down or around the room Maintain steady eye contact to show engagement
- **Minimize Distracting Gestures:** Avoid excessive hand movements or fidgeting

Don't Speak Negatively About Past Employers : Speaking negatively about past employers or colleagues can reflect poorly on your professionalism and attitude

- **Focus on Positive Experiences:** Emphasize what you learned and how you grew from past roles
- **Avoid Complaints:** Refrain from complaining or speaking negatively about previous jobs or coworkers

Don't Provide Vague or Rambling Answers : Vague or rambling answers can confuse the interviewer and dilute your message

- **Be Specific:** Use specific examples to illustrate your skills and experiences
- **Structure Responses:** Use the STAR method to provide clear and concise answers

Don't Interrupt or Dominate the Conversation : Interrupting or dominating the conversation can come across as rude or overly aggressive

- **Wait Your Turn:** Let the interviewer finish speaking before you respond
- **Balance Participation:** Engage in the conversation without monopolizing it Listen actively and respond thoughtfully

Don't Focus Solely on Salary and Benefits : Focusing too much on salary and benefits can suggest that you are more interested in compensation than the role itself

- **Balance Your Questions:** Include questions about the company's culture, goals, and how you can contribute
- **Show Genuine Interest:** Demonstrate that you are interested in the role and the company, not just the compensation

Chapter-7

Interview Questions & Answers

1. About you

1. **Tell us about yourself**

Interviewer Purpose: To get an overview of the candidate's background, including education, work experience, and personal interests This helps the interviewer assess if the candidate's profile aligns with the job requirements

Applicant's Answer: I am a recent graduate with a degree in Business Administration from XYZ University During my studies, I developed a strong foundation in project management and marketing through various internships and class projects For instance, I interned at ABC Corporation, where I assisted in launching a new product line that resulted in a 20% increase in sales I am passionate about learning new skills and have recently completed a certification in digital marketing In my free time, I enjoy volunteering at local community centers, which has helped me develop strong organizational and interpersonal skills

- ✓ **Tips:**
- ✓ Be concise and focus on relevant experiences,
- ✓ Highlight unique skills or achievements
- ✓ Show enthusiasm and a willingness to learn

2. **Why should we hire you?**

Interviewer Purpose: To determine how the candidate's skills and experiences align with the job requirements and how they can contribute to the company's success

Applicant's Answer: You should hire me because I bring a combination of strong technical skills, hands-on experience, and a passion for continuous improvement In my previous role at DEF Company, I implemented a new data analysis process that reduced reporting time by 30% My ability to analyze complex data and provide actionable insights has been recognized by my peers and supervisors I am confident that my proactive approach and ability to adapt to new challenges will make me a valuable asset to your team

- ✓ **Tips:**
- ✓ Focus on specific skills and achievements relevant to the job.
- ✓ Demonstrate how your background aligns with the company's needs
- ✓ Convey confidence and readiness to contribute

3. Can you explain these gaps in your resume?

Interviewer Purpose: To understand the reasons behind any employment gaps and assess if they were due to reasonable and productive activities.

Applicant's Answer: During the gap in my resume, I took time off to care for a family member who was ill This experience taught me valuable lessons in time management, empathy, and resilience I also used this period to take online courses in my field to stay updated with industry trends and enhance my skills Now, I am fully ready to re-enter the workforce with a renewed perspective and enhanced capabilities

- ✓ **Tips:**
- ✓ Be honest and straightforward about the reason for the gap
- ✓ Highlight any constructive activities undertaken during the gap
- ✓ Emphasize readiness and enthusiasm to return to work

4. Where do you think you'll be in five years?

Interviewer Purpose: To gauge the candidate's long-term goals and see if they align with the company's future plans

Applicant's Answer: In five years, I see myself growing within this company, taking on more responsibilities and advancing to a leadership position where I can contribute to strategic decision-making I aim to develop a deep understanding of our industry and continuously improve my skills through professional development opportunities Ultimately, I want to be a key player in driving the company's success and innovation

- ✓ **Tips:**
- ✓ Align your goals with the company's vision
- ✓ Show ambition and a commitment to growth
- ✓ Demonstrate a long-term interest in the company

5. **Why are you interested in this position?**

Interviewer Purpose: To understand the candidate's motivations and see if they have a genuine interest in the role and the company

Applicant's Answer: I am particularly interested in this position because it offers the opportunity to leverage my expertise in marketing while working in an innovative and dynamic environment I have always admired your company's commitment to creativity and excellence, and I believe my skills in digital marketing and project management can contribute significantly to your team I am excited about the potential to work on cutting-edge campaigns and collaborate with talented professionals

- ✓ **Tips:**
- ✓ Highlight specific aspects of the job that excite you
- ✓ Demonstrate knowledge about the company
- ✓ Connect your skills and interests to the role

6. **What is your biggest professional regret, and what did you learn from it?**

Interviewer Purpose: To assess the candidate's self-awareness, ability to learn from mistakes, and resilience

Applicant's Answer: My biggest professional regret is not taking the opportunity to lead a major project early in my career due to a lack of confidence This experience taught me the importance of stepping out of my comfort zone and seizing opportunities for growth Since then, I have proactively sought leadership roles and challenges, which have significantly developed my skills and confidence This regret has ultimately made me a stronger and more determined professional

- ✓ **Tips:**
- ✓ Be honest and reflective about the regret
- ✓ Focus on the lessons learned and personal growth
- ✓ Show how the experience has positively influenced your career

7. **What makes you unique?**

Interviewer Purpose: To identify unique qualities or experiences that set the candidate apart from other applicants

Applicant's Answer: What makes me unique is my interdisciplinary background in both engineering and marketing This combination allows me to approach problems with a technical mindset while also considering the customer's perspective For instance, in my previous role, I successfully bridged the gap between the technical team and the marketing department, resulting in a product launch that was both innovative and customer-centric

- ✓ **Tips:**
- ✓ Highlight a unique combination of skills or experiences
- ✓ Provide specific examples that demonstrate your uniqueness
- ✓ Relate your uniqueness to the needs of the job

8. Why do you want to work at this company?

Interviewer Purpose: To determine if the candidate has done their research on the company and if their values align with the company's culture and goals.

Applicant's Answer: I want to work at this company because of its outstanding reputation for innovation and excellence in the industry Your commitment to sustainability and community involvement resonates with my personal values I am particularly impressed by your recent projects in renewable energy, which align with my background in environmental engineering I believe that my skills and passion for sustainable development will contribute to your mission of creating a better future

- ✓ **Tips:**
- ✓ Show that you have researched the company.
- ✓ Align your values and interests with the company's mission.
- ✓ Highlight how your skills can contribute to the company's goals

9. What interests you about this role?

Interviewer Purpose: To understand what specific aspects of the job appeal to the candidate and if they have a genuine interest in the position

Applicant's Answer: I am particularly interested in this role because it offers the chance to work on innovative projects that challenge my problem-solving skills The opportunity to collaborate with a diverse team and contribute to high-impact initiatives excites me Additionally, the role's focus on developing and implementing new strategies aligns perfectly with my background in project management and my passion for continuous improvement

- ✓ **Tips:** Highlight specific responsibilities or projects that excite you.
- ✓ Connect your background and skills to the role

10. What motivates you?

Interviewer Purpose: To understand what drives the candidate and if their motivations align with the company's culture and the role's demands

Applicant's Answer: I am motivated by the opportunity to solve complex problems and make a meaningful impact I thrive in environments where I can use my analytical skills to develop innovative solutions Additionally, working as part of a collaborative team and seeing the tangible results of our efforts motivates me to continuously strive for excellence The chance to learn and grow within a company that values creativity and innovation is a significant motivator for me

- ✓ **Tips:** Identify what drives you and relate it to the job.
- ✓ Provide examples of how your motivations have influenced your work
- ✓ Show alignment between your motivations and the company's culture

11. What are your greatest strengths?

Interviewer Purpose: To identify the candidate's key strengths and see how they align with the job requirements

Applicant's Answer: My greatest strengths are my analytical thinking and problem-solving abilities I have a knack for breaking down complex issues and finding efficient solutions, which has been particularly valuable in my previous role as a data analyst Additionally, I have strong communication skills that allow me to convey technical information clearly to non-technical stakeholders These strengths enable me to contribute effectively to team projects and drive successful outcomes

- ✓ **Tips:** Focus on strengths relevant to the job.
- ✓ Provide specific examples to illustrate your strengths
- ✓ Highlight how your strengths benefit the team and company

12. What are your greatest weaknesses?

Interviewer Purpose: To assess the candidate's self-awareness and willingness to improve

Applicant's Answer: One of my greatest weaknesses is my tendency to be overly critical of my own work While this drives me to produce high-quality results, it can also lead to unnecessary stress I have been working on this by setting realistic standards for myself and seeking feedback from colleagues to gain different perspectives This has helped me balance my high standards with a healthier approach to work

- ✓ **Tips:**
- ✓ Be honest about a genuine weakness
- ✓ Explain the steps you are taking to improve
- ✓ Show how you have made progress in overcoming this weakness

13. What are your goals for the future?

Interviewer Purpose: To understand the candidate's long-term career aspirations and see if they align with the company's goals

Applicant's Answer: My long-term goal is to develop my skills in project management and eventually lead large-scale initiatives within a forward-thinking company I aim to continue expanding my knowledge in this field through professional development and practical experience In the future, I aspire to hold a leadership position where I can mentor others and contribute to the strategic direction of the organization

- ✓ **Tips:**
- ✓ Align your goals with the company's future
- ✓ Show ambition and a commitment to growth
- ✓ Demonstrate a clear plan for achieving your goals

14. How do you stay organized?

Interviewer Purpose: To assess the candidate's organizational skills and their ability to manage multiple tasks efficiently

Applicant's Answer: I stay organized by using a combination of digital tools and time management techniques I rely on project management software to track tasks and deadlines, and I prioritize my work using the

Eisenhower Matrix Additionally, I set aside time each morning to plan my day and review my goals for the week This approach helps me stay focused and ensures that I meet all my deadlines

- ✓ **Tips:**
- ✓ Describe your organizational methods and tools
- ✓ Provide examples of how these methods have helped you
- ✓ Emphasize the importance of planning and prioritization

15. What did you like most about your last position?

Interviewer Purpose: To understand what aspects of the candidate's previous job they enjoyed and if those aspects are present in the new role

Applicant's Answer: What I liked most about my last position was the collaborative team environment I enjoyed working with colleagues from different departments to achieve common goals The role also provided opportunities for continuous learning and professional development, which I found very fulfilling The supportive culture and the chance to contribute to meaningful projects were significant factors in my job satisfaction

- ✓ **Tips:**
- ✓ Highlight positive aspects relevant to the new role
- ✓ Show appreciation for teamwork and learning opportunities
- ✓ Relate your positive experiences to the company's culture

16. What did you like least about your last position?

Interviewer Purpose: To see how the candidate handles dissatisfaction and if they can provide constructive feedback

Applicant's Answer: While I appreciated many aspects of my last position, one thing I liked least was the limited opportunity for career advancement The organizational structure was quite flat, which meant that despite my eagerness to take on more responsibility, there were few avenues for growth However, this experience motivated me to seek roles where I can grow and develop professionally, which is why I am excited about this opportunity

- ✓ **Tips:** Be honest but diplomatic about dislikes
- ✓ Focus on constructive feedback,
- ✓ Relate your answer to your career goals

17. Can you tell me about a difficult work situation and how you overcame it?

Interviewer Purpose: To evaluate the candidate's problem-solving skills and resilience in challenging situations

Applicant's Answer: In my previous role, we faced a significant issue when a major project fell behind schedule due to unforeseen technical challenges I took the initiative to organize a series of brainstorming sessions with the team to identify the root causes and develop a recovery plan By reallocating resources and adjusting timelines, we managed to get the project back on track and successfully meet our deadlines This experience taught me the importance of proactive problem-solving and teamwork

- ✓ **Tips:**
- ✓ Describe the situation and your role in addressing it
- ✓ Highlight the steps taken to overcome the challenge
- ✓ Emphasize the positive outcome and lessons learned

18. How do you respond to stress or change?

Interviewer Purpose: To assess the candidate's ability to handle stress and adapt to change, both of which are common in dynamic work environments

Applicant's Answer: I respond to stress and change by staying focused and maintaining a positive attitude I prioritize tasks and break them down into manageable steps to avoid feeling overwhelmed When faced with change, I remain flexible and open to new ideas In my previous role, during a major organizational restructuring, I adapted quickly by learning new processes and supporting my team through the transition This approach helped us maintain productivity and morale

- ✓ **Tips:**
- ✓ Highlight your ability to stay calm and focused.
- ✓ Provide examples of successful adaptation to change.
- ✓ Emphasize the importance of flexibility and a positive attitude

19. How do you handle conflict at work?

Interviewer Purpose: To understand the candidate's conflict resolution skills and their approach to maintaining a harmonious work environment

Applicant's Answer: When handling conflict at work, I believe in addressing the issue directly and diplomatically I always start by listening to the other person's perspective to understand their concerns fully Then, I aim to find common ground and work towards a mutually beneficial solution In my previous job, I successfully mediated a disagreement between two team members by facilitating open communication and helping them see each other's viewpoints

- ✓ **Tips:**
- ✓ Emphasize the importance of listening and understanding.
- ✓ Provide examples of successful conflict resolution
- ✓ Highlight your focus on finding mutually beneficial solutions

20. What is your greatest accomplishment?

Interviewer Purpose: To identify significant achievements in the candidate's career and understand what they value as success

Applicant's Answer: My greatest accomplishment was leading a cross-functional team to develop and launch a new software product within a tight deadline The project required extensive coordination between different departments, and we faced several technical challenges along the way However, through effective leadership and collaboration, we not only met the deadline but also received positive feedback from our clients This accomplishment demonstrated my ability to lead and deliver results under pressure

- ✓ **Tips:**
- ✓ Choose an accomplishment that is relevant to the job
- ✓ Describe the challenges and your role in achieving success
- ✓ Highlight the positive impact of the accomplishment

21. How do you define success?

Interviewer Purpose: To understand the candidate's values and how they measure their achievements

Applicant's Answer: I define success as achieving goals that contribute to both personal growth and the organization's objectives Success means continuously improving my skills, taking on new challenges, and making a positive impact on my team and the company It also involves maintaining a healthy work-life balance and finding fulfillment in my work For me, true success is a combination of professional accomplishments and personal satisfaction

- ✓ **Tips:**
- ✓ Provide a balanced view of success, including personal and professional aspects
- ✓ Highlight the importance of continuous improvement
- ✓ Relate your definition of success to the company's goals

22. How do your skills align with this role?

Interviewer Purpose: To see if the candidate's skills match the job requirements and how they can contribute to the company

Applicant's Answer: My skills align well with this role because of my extensive experience in project management and my strong analytical abilities I have successfully managed multiple projects from inception to completion, ensuring they were delivered on time and within budget Additionally, my proficiency in data analysis allows me to make informed decisions and provide valuable insights These skills, combined with my ability to collaborate effectively with cross-functional teams, make me a strong fit for this position

Tips:

- ✓ Match your skills with the key responsibilities of the role
- ✓ Provide specific examples to illustrate your capabilities
- ✓ Highlight your ability to contribute to the company's success

23. What do you value most in a workplace?

Interviewer Purpose: To understand the candidate's workplace preferences and see if they align with the company's culture

Applicant's Answer: I value a workplace that fosters collaboration, innovation, and continuous learning Being part of a team that encourages open communication and values diverse perspectives is important to me Additionally, I appreciate an environment that offers opportunities for professional development and supports work-life balance These elements contribute to my productivity and job satisfaction, and I believe they are essential for a thriving and successful workplace

- ✓ **Tips:** Highlight values that align with the company's culture
- ✓ Emphasize the importance of teamwork and professional growth
- ✓ Relate your preferences to your productivity and satisfaction

24. Why are you leaving your current job?

Interviewer Purpose: To understand the candidate's reasons for seeking a new position and ensure they are leaving their previous job for positive and professional reasons.

Applicant's Answer: I am leaving my current job because I am seeking new challenges and opportunities for growth that align more closely with my career goals While I have gained valuable experience in my current role, I believe that your company offers the innovative environment and professional development opportunities that I am looking for I am excited about the chance to contribute my skills to a new team and continue growing professionally

- ✓ **Tips:**
- ✓ Focus on positive reasons for leaving
- ✓ Emphasize your desire for growth and new challenges
- ✓ Avoid negative comments about your current employer

25. What is your salary range expectation?

Interviewer Purpose: To understand the candidate's salary expectations and ensure they align with the company's budget.

Applicant's Answer: Based on my research and understanding of the industry standards, I believe a fair salary range for this position would be between $60,000 and $70,000 per year However, I am open to discussing this further and am willing to negotiate based on the overall compensation package, including benefits and opportunities for professional development

- ✓ **Tips:**
- ✓ Provide a researched and reasonable salary range
- ✓ Show willingness to negotiate
- ✓ Consider the entire compensation package, not just salary

26. Do you have any questions?

Interviewer Purpose: To gauge the candidate's interest in the role and their understanding of the company

Applicant's Answer: Yes, I do have a few questions Could you tell me more about the team I would be working with and the current projects they are working on? Additionally, what are the opportunities for professional development within the company? Lastly, how does the company support work-life balance for its employees?

- ✓ **Tips:**
- ✓ Prepare thoughtful questions in advance
- ✓ Focus on topics like team structure, projects, and professional growth
- ✓ Show genuine interest in the company and role

27. What are you passionate about?

Interviewer Purpose: To understand what drives the candidate and if their passions align with the company's values and culture

Applicant's Answer: I am passionate about using technology to solve real-world problems I find great satisfaction in developing innovative solutions that improve efficiency and make a positive impact In my free time, I enjoy working on personal coding projects and staying updated with the latest tech trends This passion for technology and problem-solving aligns well with the innovative spirit of your company and the role I am applying for

- ✓ **Tips:** Highlight a passion relevant to the job or industry
- ✓ Provide examples of how this passion influences your work
- ✓ Show enthusiasm and a commitment to continuous learning

28. Tell me about your work experience

Interviewer Purpose: To get a comprehensive understanding of the candidate's professional background and relevant experience

Applicant's Answer: I have over five years of experience in the marketing field, specializing in digital marketing and campaign management In my previous role at XYZ Company, I led a team that executed multi-channel marketing campaigns, resulting in a 25% increase in customer engagement I have experience in SEO, content marketing, and data analysis, which have helped me develop strategies that drive results My hands-on approach and ability to adapt to changing market trends have been key to my success

- ✓ **Tips:**
- ✓ Provide a summary of your most relevant experiences
- ✓ Highlight key achievements and skills
- ✓ Relate your experience to the job you are applying for

29. How do you work under pressure?

Interviewer Purpose: To assess the candidate's ability to maintain performance and composure in high-stress situations

Applicant's Answer: I thrive under pressure by staying organized and focused on the task at hand I prioritize my work, set realistic deadlines, and break down complex tasks into manageable steps In my previous role, I successfully managed multiple high-pressure projects by maintaining open communication with my team and staying adaptable to changes This approach has helped me deliver quality results even in challenging situations

- ✓ **Tips:**
- ✓ Highlight your organizational skills and ability to prioritize
- ✓ Provide examples of successful work under pressure
- ✓ Emphasize the importance of communication and adaptability

30. What is your dream job?

Interviewer Purpose: To understand the candidate's long-term career aspirations and see if they align with the company's opportunities

Applicant's Answer: My dream job is one where I can combine my passion for technology and innovation with leadership opportunities I aspire to lead a team of talented professionals in developing cutting-edge solutions that make a significant impact on the industry I am particularly interested in roles that offer continuous learning and the chance to drive strategic initiatives This aligns with the innovative and forward-thinking culture of your company

- ✓ **Tips:**
- ✓ Describe a role that aligns with your skills and passions
- ✓ Highlight leadership and continuous learning opportunities
- ✓ Relate your dream job to the company's vision and values

31. What can you bring to the company?

Interviewer Purpose: To understand the candidate's unique value proposition and how they can contribute to the company's success

Applicant's Answer: I bring a strong background in data analysis and project management, along with a proactive and solution-oriented mindset My ability to analyze complex data and develop actionable insights has helped previous employers make informed decisions and improve efficiency Additionally, my experience in leading cross-functional teams ensures that I can collaborate effectively and drive successful project outcomes I am confident that my skills and approach will contribute positively to your company's goals

- ✓ **Tips:**
- ✓ Highlight unique skills and experiences relevant to the role
- ✓ Provide examples of past contributions and successes
- ✓ Show enthusiasm for contributing to the company's success

32. How do you handle constructive criticism?

Interviewer Purpose: To assess the candidate's openness to feedback and their ability to use it for personal and professional growth

Applicant's Answer: I handle constructive criticism by viewing it as an opportunity for growth I listen carefully to the feedback, ask clarifying questions if needed, and reflect on how I can improve For example, when my supervisor suggested I work on my presentation skills, I took a public speaking course and sought opportunities to present in team meetings This feedback helped me become more confident and effective in communicating my ideas

- ✓ **Tips:**
- ✓ Show a positive attitude towards feedback
- ✓ Provide an example of how you used criticism to improve
- ✓ Emphasize your commitment to continuous learning and development

33. What is your preferred work style?

Interviewer Purpose: To understand the candidate's work preferences and see if they align with the company's work environment and culture

Applicant's Answer: My preferred work style is collaborative and goal-oriented I enjoy working in teams where we can share ideas and leverage each other's strengths to achieve common goals I am also highly organized and thrive in environments where I can plan my tasks and manage my time effectively Flexibility and open communication are key aspects of my work style, which help me adapt to changing priorities and stay aligned with the team's objectives

- ✓ **Tips:**
- ✓ Highlight aspects of your work style that align with the company's culture
- ✓ Provide examples of how your work style has contributed to success
- ✓ Emphasize the importance of flexibility and communication

2. Education Based Questions

1. Explain Your Education Gaps in Your CV?

Interviewer Purpose: To understand the reasons behind any breaks in your education and ensure they reflect a candidate's reliability and dedication.

Applicant's Answer: During the gaps in my education, I took time to gain practical experience and explore my interests through internships and part-time jobs This period allowed me to develop valuable skills and clarify my career goals For example, I interned at a tech startup where I gained hands-on experience in software development, which reinforced my passion for the field and made me more certain about my career path

- ✓ **Tips:**
- ✓ Be honest and provide constructive reasons for the gaps
- ✓ Highlight any skills or experiences gained during this period
- ✓ Emphasize how the gap contributed to your career development

2. Explain the Reason for Less Marks / Percentage / CGPA in Your Education

Interviewer Purpose: To understand any factors that may have affected the candidate's academic performance and ensure they are capable of handling job responsibilities.

Applicant's Answer: My lower marks can be attributed to my involvement in several extracurricular activities that sometimes took up a significant portion of my time While my academic performance may have suffered slightly, these experiences taught me valuable skills such as time management, teamwork, and leadership I believe these skills are crucial for professional success and have prepared me well for this role

- ✓ **Tips:**
- ✓ Be honest and constructive about the reasons for lower marks
- ✓ Highlight the skills and experiences gained from extracurricular activities
- ✓ Emphasize how these experiences have prepared you for the job

3. What is the reason that you are not a topper in your course?

Interviewer Purpose: To assess the candidate's perspective on academic performance and its impact on their professional capabilities

Applicant's Answer: While I was not the top student in my course, I prioritized a well-rounded education that included practical experience, internships, and extracurricular activities This approach allowed me to develop a broader skill set and gain real-world experience, which I believe is equally important as academic excellence These experiences have equipped me with a diverse set of skills that I can bring to this role

- ✓ **Tips:**
- ✓ Emphasize a balanced approach to education
- ✓ Highlight the importance of practical experience and extracurricular activities
- ✓ Show how these experiences contribute to your professional skills

4. How Did You Balance Your Academic Responsibilities with Extracurricular Activities?

Interviewer Purpose: To evaluate the candidate's time management skills and their ability to handle multiple responsibilities effectively

Applicant's Answer: Balancing academics and extracurricular activities required effective time management and prioritization I created a schedule that allocated specific times for studying and participating in activities Additionally, I set clear goals for both areas and regularly reviewed my progress to ensure I stayed on track This approach helped me maintain a good academic record while also developing leadership and teamwork skills through extracurricular involvement

- ✓ **Tips:**
- ✓ Highlight your time management and prioritization strategies
- ✓ Provide examples of how you successfully balanced both areas
- ✓ Emphasize the skills gained from this balance

5. What Influenced Your Choice of Major, and How Do You See It Aligning with Your Career Goals?

Interviewer Purpose: To understand the candidate's motivation behind choosing their major and how it aligns with their career aspirations

Applicant's Answer: My choice of major in computer science was influenced by my fascination with technology and problem-solving I have always enjoyed coding and developing software, which led me to pursue this field My career goal is to become a software engineer, and my major has provided me with a strong foundation in programming, algorithms, and system design This knowledge aligns perfectly with my aspirations and the requirements of this role

- ✓ **Tips:**
- ✓ Explain your passion and interest in the subject
- ✓ Highlight how your major has prepared you for your career goals
- ✓ Show alignment between your education and the job role

6. What Are the Reasons That You Have Scored Less in Theory Exams and More in Practical Examinations?

Interviewer Purpose: To understand the candidate's strengths and weaknesses in different aspects of their education

Applicant's Answer: I scored higher in practical exams because I excel in hands-on learning and applying theoretical concepts to real-world scenarios Practical exams allowed me to demonstrate my skills and understanding through tangible results On the other hand, theory exams required rote memorization, which is not my strongest suit However, my ability to perform well in practical exams highlights my competence in applying knowledge effectively

- ✓ **Tips:**
- ✓ Highlight your strengths in practical applications
- ✓ Explain how practical skills are valuable in the job role
- ✓ Show willingness to improve theoretical knowledge

7. What Are the Reasons That You Have Scored Less in Practical Exams and More in Theory Examinations?

Interviewer Purpose: To understand the candidate's strengths and weaknesses in different aspects of their education

Applicant's Answer: I scored higher in theory exams because I have a strong aptitude for understanding and retaining theoretical concepts My analytical and critical thinking skills helped me excel in written examinations However, I recognize the importance of practical skills and have been working on improving my hands-on experience through internships and personal projects This balance of theoretical knowledge and practical application is crucial for success in this role

- ✓ **Tips:** Highlight your strengths in theoretical understanding
- ✓ Explain steps taken to improve practical skills
- ✓ Emphasize the importance of balancing both aspects in the job

8. What Do Your Teachers Describe About You?

Interviewer Purpose: To gain insights into the candidate's character, work ethic, and abilities from a third-party perspective

Applicant's Answer: My teachers would describe me as a diligent, curious, and proactive student They often praised my dedication to learning and my ability to tackle complex problems with a methodical approach Additionally, they appreciated my willingness to assist classmates and contribute to group projects, highlighting my teamwork and leadership skills

- ✓ **Tips:**
- ✓ Highlight positive attributes and feedback from teachers
- ✓ Provide specific examples of praise received
- ✓ Relate these attributes to the job role

9. Your Education Is Different and Job Roles Are Different Justify the Same

Interviewer Purpose: To understand how the candidate can apply their educational background to a role that may not be directly related

Applicant's Answer: Although my education is in liberal arts, I have developed strong analytical, communication, and research skills that are highly transferable to this role in marketing My ability to understand and interpret complex information, coupled with my creativity and writing skills, enables me to create compelling marketing campaigns Additionally, my experience in project management and teamwork during my studies has prepared me to contribute effectively to your team

- ✓ **Tips:** Highlight transferable skills from your education
- ✓ Provide examples of how these skills apply to the job role
- ✓ Emphasize your ability to adapt and learn quickly

10. Can You Describe Your Educational Background and How It Has Prepared You for This Role?

Interviewer Purpose: To assess the relevance of the candidate's educational background to the job role and understand how it has prepared them for the position

Applicant's Answer: I hold a degree in business administration, with a focus on marketing My coursework included subjects like consumer behavior, digital marketing, and strategic management, which provided me with a solid foundation in marketing principles Additionally, my internships allowed me to apply theoretical knowledge to real-world scenarios, honing my skills in campaign management and market analysis This combination of education and practical experience has prepared me well for this role in your company

- ✓ **Tips:**
- ✓ Highlight relevant coursework and experiences
- ✓ Explain how your education aligns with the job role
- ✓ Provide examples of practical applications of your knowledge

11. What Was Your Most Challenging Course During Your Studies, and How Did You Overcome It?

Interviewer Purpose: To understand the candidate's problem-solving skills and perseverance in the face of academic challenges
Applicant's Answer: The most challenging course during my studies was advanced calculus The complexity of the concepts and the pace of the course required me to adopt new study techniques I formed a study group with classmates, attended additional tutoring sessions, and dedicated extra hours to practice problems Through these efforts, I was able to grasp the material better and successfully pass the course, demonstrating my commitment to overcoming challenges

- ✓ **Tips:**
- ✓ Identify the challenging course and explain why it was difficult
- ✓ Describe the strategies used to overcome the challenge
- ✓ Emphasize the lessons learned and how they apply to your professional skills

12. Can You Share an Example of a Project You Worked on During Your Education That Is Relevant to This Position?

Interviewer Purpose: To assess the candidate's practical experience and how it relates to the job role

Applicant's Answer: During my final year, I worked on a project that involved developing a digital marketing strategy for a local business We conducted market research, identified target demographics, and created a comprehensive plan that included SEO, social media marketing, and email campaigns This project allowed me to apply theoretical knowledge to a real-world situation and develop practical skills in digital marketing, which are directly relevant to this role

- ✓ **Tips:** Choose a project that is closely related to the job role
- ✓ Explain the project's objectives, your role, and the outcome
- ✓ Highlight the skills and knowledge gained from the project

13. Can You Discuss a Time When You Had to Collaborate on a Group Project During Your Studies?

Interviewer Purpose: To evaluate the candidate's teamwork and collaboration skills

Applicant's Answer: In my marketing class, we were assigned a group project to create a marketing plan for a new product Our team had diverse strengths, and I took on the role of coordinating our efforts and ensuring effective communication We held regular meetings, divided tasks based on individual strengths, and used collaborative tools to track progress This experience taught me the importance of clear communication, delegation, and teamwork, which are essential skills for this role.

- ✓ **Tips:** Describe the group project and your role in it,
- ✓ Highlight the importance of communication and collaboration,
- ✓ emphasize the positive outcome and lessons learned

14. Can you Describe Any Leadership Roles You Held During Your Education?

Interviewer Purpose: To assess the candidate's leadership experience and potential

Applicant's Answer: During my final year, I was elected as the president of the student council In this role, I organized events, led meetings, and represented the student body in discussions with the administration This position required strong organizational and interpersonal skills, as well as the ability to make decisions under pressure My leadership experience has equipped me with the skills to lead projects and teams effectively, which I believe will be valuable in this role

- ✓ **Tips:**
- ✓ Describe the leadership role and your responsibilities
- ✓ Highlight the skills and experiences gained
- ✓ Relate these skills to the job role

15. Can You Explain How a Particular Course or Professor Influenced Your Career Path?

Interviewer Purpose: To understand the impact of the candidate's educational experiences on their career choices

Applicant's Answer: My professor in digital marketing had a profound influence on my career path Their passion for the subject and real-world insights inspired me to pursue a career in marketing The course projects and case studies provided practical knowledge and skills that I found fascinating and motivating This experience solidified my decision to specialize in digital marketing and seek opportunities in this field

- ✓ **Tips:**
- ✓ Identify the course or professor and explain their influence
- ✓ Highlight the specific aspects that inspired you
- ✓ Explain how this influence shaped your career decisions

3. Organization based Questions

1. **What Do You Know About This Company/Organization?**

Interviewer Purpose: To assess whether the candidate has researched the company and understands its mission, values, and industry position

Applicant's Answer: I have researched your company extensively and am impressed by your commitment to innovation and customer satisfaction Your recent expansion into international markets and the launch of eco-friendly products demonstrate your dedication to sustainability and growth I am particularly drawn to your collaborative work culture and community involvement, which align with my personal values and professional aspirations

- ✓ **Tips:**
- ✓ Research the company thoroughly before the interview
- ✓ Highlight specific aspects that align with your values
- ✓ Show enthusiasm and genuine interest in the company

2. **How Did You Hear About This Position?**

Interviewer Purpose: To understand how the candidate found the job opening and to gauge their level of interest and initiative

Applicant's Answer: I came across this position on your company's LinkedIn page I have been following your company for a while due to my interest in your innovative projects and positive workplace culture When I saw the job posting, I was immediately excited about the opportunity to contribute to your team

- ✓ **Tips:**
- ✓ Mention the source where you found the job
- ✓ Express your ongoing interest in the company
- ✓ Highlight your enthusiasm for the position

3. **Why did you decide to apply for this position?**

Interviewer Purpose: To understand the candidate's motivations and how well they align with the role and company

Applicant's Answer: I applied for this position because it perfectly aligns with my skills and career aspirations Your company's focus on cutting-edge technology and continuous improvement resonates with my passion for innovation I am excited about the opportunity to contribute to your projects and grow professionally in an environment that values creativity and collaboration

- ✓ **Tips:**
- ✓ Explain how the role aligns with your skills and career goals
- ✓ Highlight aspects of the company that attracted you
- ✓ Show enthusiasm for contributing to the company

4. Why Do You Want to Work Here?

Interviewer Purpose: To gauge the candidate's interest in the company and their cultural fit

Applicant's Answer: I am drawn to your company because of its reputation for fostering a supportive and inclusive work environment I admire your commitment to employee development and community engagement The opportunity to work with a team that values innovation and collaboration is very appealing to me, and I believe my background in project management will allow me to make a meaningful contribution to your ongoing success

- ✓ **Tips:**
- ✓ Highlight the company's positive attributes
- ✓ Explain how these align with your values and career goals
- ✓ Show enthusiasm for joining the team

5. What is Your Greatest Accomplishment?

Interviewer Purpose: To understand the candidate's proudest professional achievements and what they consider significant.

Applicant's Answer: My greatest accomplishment was leading a team to develop a new software application that streamlined our company's workflow This project required coordinating multiple departments, managing tight deadlines, and overcoming technical challenges The application not only improved efficiency by 30% but also received positive feedback from users, highlighting my ability to lead and deliver impactful projects

- ✓ **Tips:**
- ✓ Choose an accomplishment relevant to the job
- ✓ Highlight the impact and positive feedback
- ✓ Explain the skills and qualities demonstrated

6. What Motivates You in Your Professional Life?

Interviewer Purpose: To understand what drives the candidate and ensure their motivations align with the job role

Applicant's Answer: I am motivated by the challenge of solving complex problems and the satisfaction of seeing the tangible results of my work I thrive in environments that encourage continuous learning and innovation Additionally, being part of a collaborative team that works towards common goals energizes me and drives me to perform at my best

- ✓ **Tips:**
- ✓ Identify what genuinely drives you
- ✓ Relate it to the job role and company culture
- ✓ Highlight your passion for continuous improvement

7. What Skills Are You Currently Working on Improving?

Interviewer Purpose: To gauge the candidate's commitment to professional development and their self-awareness

Applicant's Answer: I am currently focusing on improving my data analysis skills, particularly in using advanced analytics tools like Python and R I have enrolled in online courses and am working on projects to apply these skills in real-world scenarios Enhancing my data analysis capabilities will allow me to contribute more effectively to data-driven decision-making processes in this role

Tips:

- ✓ Identify a relevant skill you are improving
- ✓ Mention the steps you are taking to improve it
- ✓ Explain how this skill will benefit the job role

8. What are you looking for In a new position?

Interviewer Purpose: To understand the candidate's expectations and ensure the role aligns with their career goals

Applicant's Answer: In a new position, I am looking for opportunities to grow professionally and take on challenging projects I value a supportive and collaborative work environment where I can contribute my skills and learn from others Additionally, I seek a role that allows me to make a meaningful impact and aligns with my long-term career aspirations

- ✓ **Tips:**
- ✓ Identify what you value in a job
- ✓ Explain how it aligns with your career goals
- ✓ Relate it to the company and role you are applying for

9. Can You Describe Your Ideal Job?

Interviewer Purpose: To understand the candidate's career aspirations and see if the role matches their ideal job

Applicant's Answer: My ideal job involves a combination of creative problem-solving, collaboration with a talented team, and opportunities for continuous learning I thrive in roles that allow me to take on challenging projects and make a meaningful impact Additionally, a company culture that values innovation, diversity, and professional development is essential to me

- ✓ **Tips:**
- ✓ Describe the elements of your ideal job
- ✓ Relate these elements to the role you are applying for
- ✓ Highlight the importance of company culture

10. Are You Considering Other Positions at Other Companies?

Interviewer Purpose: To gauge the candidate's job search activity and interest level

Applicant's Answer: Yes, I am exploring multiple opportunities to find the best fit for my skills and career goals However, I am particularly interested in this position because of your company's innovative projects and supportive work environment I believe this role aligns perfectly with my professional aspirations and offers the growth opportunities I am seeking

- ✓ **Tips:**
- ✓ Be honest about considering other opportunities
- ✓ Highlight your particular interest in the current role
- ✓ Emphasize how it aligns with your career goals

11. What is the Professional Achievement You're Most Proud of?

Interviewer Purpose: To understand the candidate's proudest professional achievements and what they consider significant

Applicant's Answer: I am most proud of leading a successful product launch that exceeded our sales targets by 20% This achievement required extensive market research, strategic planning, and effective team collaboration The positive customer feedback and the financial success of the product reinforced my skills in project management and marketing

- ✓ **Tips:**
- ✓ Choose an achievement relevant to the job
- ✓ Highlight the impact and positive feedback
- ✓ Explain the skills and qualities demonstrated

12. What Kind of Working Environment Do You Work Best In?

Interviewer Purpose: To determine if the candidate will thrive in the company's work environment

Applicant's Answer: I work best in a collaborative and dynamic environment where innovation is encouraged, and continuous learning is supported I value open communication and a team-oriented culture that fosters creativity and mutual respect Such an environment motivates me to perform at my best and contribute effectively to team goals

- ✓ **Tips:**
- ✓ Describe your ideal work environment
- ✓ Relate it to the company's culture
- ✓ Highlight how this environment enhances your performance

13. What Are Your Career Goals?

Interviewer Purpose: To understand the candidate's long-term career aspirations and ensure they align with the company's objectives

Applicant's Answer: My career goal is to advance to a leadership position in project management within the next five years I aim to continue developing my skills in strategic planning and team leadership while contributing to innovative projects I believe this role provides the perfect opportunity to grow professionally and align my career trajectory with the company's vision

- ✓ **Tips:**
- ✓ Identify your long-term career goals
- ✓ Explain how the role aligns with these goals
- ✓ Highlight your commitment to professional growth

14. Explain the Reason for Less Marks / Percentage / CGPA in Your Education

Interviewer Purpose: To understand any factors that may have affected the candidate's academic performance and ensure they are capable of handling job responsibilities despite this

Applicant's Answer: My lower marks can be attributed to my involvement in several extracurricular activities that sometimes took up a significant portion of my time While my academic performance may have suffered slightly, these experiences taught me valuable skills such as time management, teamwork, and leadership I believe these skills are crucial for professional success and have prepared me well for this role

- ✓ **Tips:**
- ✓ Be honest and constructive about the reasons for lower marks
- ✓ Highlight the skills and experiences gained from extracurricular activities
- ✓ Emphasize how these experiences have prepared you for the job

15. Can You Describe Any Leadership Roles You Held During Your Education?

Interviewer Purpose: To assess the candidate's leadership experience and potential

Applicant's Answer: During my final year, I was elected as the president of the student council In this role, I organized events, led meetings, and represented the student body in discussions with the administration This position required strong organizational and interpersonal skills, as well as the ability to make decisions under pressure My leadership experience has equipped me with the skills to lead projects and teams effectively, which I believe will be valuable in this role

- ✓ **Tips:** Describe the leadership role and your responsibilities
- ✓ Highlight the skills and experiences gained
- ✓ Relate these skills to the job role

16. How Did You Balance Your Academic Responsibilities with Extracurricular Activities?

Interviewer Purpose: To assess time management and organizational skills

Applicant's Answer: Balancing academics and extracurricular activities required careful planning and prioritization I maintained a strict schedule, setting aside specific times for study and participation in activities Effective time management and discipline enabled me to excel in both areas, developing skills such as multitasking, resilience, and teamwork that are crucial for professional success

- ✓ **Tips:**
- ✓ Explain your approach to time management
- ✓ Highlight the skills developed through balancing responsibilities
- ✓ Relate these skills to the job role

17. What Influenced Your Choice of Major, and How Do You See It Aligning with Your Career Goals?

Interviewer Purpose: To understand the candidate's decision-making process and career alignment

Applicant's Answer: My choice of major in computer science was influenced by my passion for technology and problem-solving This field excites me due to its constant innovation and the potential to impact various industries My career goal is to become a software developer, and my major has provided me with a strong foundation in programming, data structures, and algorithms, which are essential for this role

- ✓ **Tips:**
- ✓ Explain your passion and decision-making process
- ✓ Highlight how your major aligns with your career goals
- ✓ Relate your educational background to the job role

18. What Are the Reasons That You Have Scored Less in Theory Exams and More in Practical Examinations?

Interviewer Purpose: To understand the candidate's strengths and areas for improvement

Applicant's Answer: My practical exam scores were higher because I excel in hands-on application and problem-solving Theory exams were more challenging due to my preference for experiential learning over rote memorization This has taught me the importance of balancing theoretical knowledge with practical skills, and I have since focused on improving my study methods to enhance my theoretical understanding

- ✓ **Tips:**
- ✓ Identify the reasons for different performance levels
- ✓ Highlight your strengths in practical application
- ✓ Explain steps taken to improve theoretical understanding

19 Can You Share an Example of a Project You Worked on During Your Education That is Relevant to This Position?

Interviewer Purpose: To assess the candidate's practical experience and relevance to the job role

Applicant's Answer: In my final year, I worked on a project to develop a mobile application for managing personal finances This project involved conducting user research, designing the interface, and coding the application It required collaboration with a team and application of my programming and project management skills The project was successful and received positive feedback for its user-friendly design, demonstrating my ability to deliver relevant and impactful work

- ✓ **Tips:**
- ✓ Describe the project and your role in it
- ✓ Highlight the skills and experiences gained
- ✓ Relate the project's success to the job role

20 What Are Your Career Goals?

Interviewer Purpose: To understand the candidate's long-term career aspirations and ensure they align with the company's objectives

Applicant's Answer: My career goal is to advance to a leadership position in project management within the next five years I aim to continue developing my skills in strategic planning and team leadership while contributing to innovative projects I believe this role provides the perfect opportunity to grow professionally and align my career trajectory with the company's vision

Tips: Identify your long-term career goals, Explain how the role aligns with these goals, Highlight your commitment to professional growth

4.Experience based Questions

1 Can You Explain Why There is a Gap in Your Employment History?

Interviewer Purpose: To understand any gaps in employment and assess the candidate's readiness to re-enter the workforce

Applicant's Answer: I took a break from my professional career to focus on personal development and address some family matters During this period, I also took courses to enhance my skills and stayed updated with industry trends I am now eager to bring my refreshed perspective and new skills to this role

Tips: Be honest and constructive about the gap, Highlight how you stayed productive during the break, ` Emphasize your readiness to re-enter the workforce

2 How Would You Describe Your Approach to Handling Pressure and Stressful Situations?

Interviewer Purpose: To assess the candidate's ability to manage stress and work under pressure

Applicant's Answer: I approach stressful situations by staying calm and focusing on solutions I prioritize tasks, delegate when necessary, and maintain open communication with my team This method has always helped me navigate pressure effectively and ensure productivity

- ✓ **Tips:**
- ✓ Highlight your ability to stay calm and focused
- ✓ Describe your prioritization and delegation strategies
- ✓ Emphasize the importance of communication

3 Why Haven't You Completed Your Degree Yet?

Interviewer Purpose: To understand the reasons behind the candidate not finishing their degree and assess their commitment to education

Applicant's Answer: I had to put my degree on hold due to unforeseen personal circumstances However, I have gained significant practical experience in the field and am committed to completing my degree part-time while continuing to advance professionally

- ✓ **Tips:**
- ✓ Be honest about the reasons for not completing your degree
- ✓ Highlight the practical experience gained in lieu of formal education
- ✓ Express your commitment to completing your degree

4 How Did You Come to the Decision to Leave Your Last Job?

Interviewer Purpose: To understand the candidate's reasons for leaving their previous job and ensure they have a positive and professional outlook

Applicant's Answer: I decided to leave my last job to seek new challenges and opportunities for growth that align better with my career goals While I appreciated my time there, I am looking for a role that offers more scope for innovation and professional development

- ✓ **Tips:**
- ✓ Focus on the positive aspects of your decision
- ✓ Emphasize your desire for growth and new challenges
- ✓ Maintain a professional tone about your previous employer

5 What Led You to Change Your Career Direction?

Interviewer Purpose: To understand the candidate's motivations for changing career paths and assess their commitment to the new field

Applicant's Answer: I realized that my true passion lies in a different field where I can leverage my skills more effectively I took courses and gained relevant experience to ensure a smooth transition This change has reinvigorated my career, and I am eager to contribute to this new industry

- ✓ **Tips:**
- ✓ Explain your passion for the new field
- ✓ Highlight the steps you took to transition smoothly
- ✓ Emphasize your commitment to the new career path

6 If Given a Choice, Would You Prefer to Innovate a Process or Adhere to Established Procedures?

Interviewer Purpose: To understand the candidate's inclination towards innovation versus following established protocols
Applicant's Answer: I believe in balancing innovation with established procedures While it's important to respect proven methods, I also enjoy identifying areas for improvement and implementing innovative solutions that can enhance efficiency and effectiveness

- ✓ **Tips:**
- ✓ Highlight the importance of both innovation and established procedures
- ✓ Give examples of when you have successfully balanced both
- ✓ Emphasize your adaptability to different scenarios

7 What Factors Contributed to Your Decision to Switch Jobs Frequently?

Interviewer Purpose: To understand the reasons behind the candidate's frequent job changes and assess their stability

Applicant's Answer: My job changes were driven by a desire to gain diverse experiences and skills in different environments Each position offered unique challenges and learning opportunities, which have collectively enhanced my professional development I am now looking for a long-term role where I can apply this diverse experience

- ✓ **Tips:**
- ✓ Explain the positive reasons behind your job changes
- ✓ Highlight the skills and experiences gained from each role
- ✓ Emphasize your commitment to finding a stable, long-term position

8 How Do You Think Your Supervisor Would Describe You?

Interviewer Purpose: To gauge the candidate's self-awareness and understand how they are perceived in a professional setting

Applicant's Answer: My supervisor would describe me as a dedicated and reliable team player with strong problem-solving skills They would also mention my ability to adapt quickly to new challenges and my proactive approach to continuous improvement

- ✓ **Tips:**
- ✓ Highlight your strengths and positive qualities
- ✓ Provide specific examples of feedback from your supervisor
- ✓ Emphasize qualities relevant to the job role

9 Are You Comfortable Working Late Hours or on Weekends?

Interviewer Purpose: To assess the candidate's flexibility and willingness to meet the demands of the job

Applicant's Answer: I understand that some roles require flexibility with working hours, and I am prepared to work late hours or weekends when necessary I value maintaining a healthy work-life balance, but I am also committed to meeting deadlines and ensuring project success

- ✓ **Tips:**
- ✓ Express your willingness to be flexible with working hours
- ✓ Emphasize the importance of work-life balance
- ✓ Highlight your commitment to meeting deadlines

10 Were There Specific Reasons Why You Were Let Go From Your Previous Job?

Interviewer Purpose: To understand the circumstances of the candidate's termination and ensure they have a positive outlook on the situation

Applicant's Answer: I was let go due to a company-wide restructuring that resulted in significant downsizing Although it was a challenging experience, it gave me an opportunity to reflect on my career goals and seek new opportunities that better align with my aspirations

- ✓ **Tips:**
- ✓ Be honest about the reasons for being let go
- ✓ Focus on the positive outcomes and learning experiences
- ✓ Maintain a professional and positive tone

11 How Would You Spend Your First 30, 60, or 90 Days in This Role?

Interviewer Purpose: To assess the candidate's plan for integrating into the new role and their proactive approach to starting a new job

Applicant's Answer: In the first 30 days, I would focus on understanding the company's processes and building relationships with my team By 60 days, I would start taking on projects and contributing to team goals By 90 days, I aim to have a thorough understanding of my role and be actively contributing to key projects, bringing measurable value to the team

- ✓ **Tips:**
- ✓ Outline a clear and structured plan
- ✓ Emphasize your proactive approach to integration
- ✓ Highlight your commitment to adding value quickly

12 Are You Someone Who Enjoys Taking Risks?

Interviewer Purpose: To understand the candidate's risk tolerance and approach to decision-making

Applicant's Answer: I am calculated when it comes to taking risks I believe in assessing the potential outcomes and benefits before making a decision This approach has allowed me to take innovative steps while minimizing unnecessary risks, leading to successful project outcomes

- ✓ **Tips:**
- ✓ Highlight your calculated approach to risk-taking
- ✓ Provide examples of successful risk-taking
- ✓ Emphasize the importance of assessing potential outcomes

13 Do You Consider Yourself a Team-Oriented Person?

Interviewer Purpose: To assess the candidate's ability to work collaboratively

Applicant's Answer: Absolutely, I thrive in team environments I believe that collaboration leads to better solutions and fosters a supportive work culture I always strive to contribute positively to the team, communicate effectively, and support my colleagues to achieve common goals

- ✓ **Tips:**
- ✓ Highlight your collaborative mindset

- ✓ Provide examples of successful teamwork
- ✓ Emphasize the benefits of a team-oriented approach

14 What's Your Opinion on the Difference Between Hard Work and Smart Work?

Interviewer Purpose: To understand the candidate's work ethic and approach to efficiency
Applicant's Answer: Hard work involves putting in the necessary effort and dedication, while smart work means finding the most efficient way to achieve results I believe in combining both approaches: working hard to develop skills and knowledge and working smart to apply them effectively and achieve optimal outcomes

- ✓ **Tips:**
- ✓ Define hard work and smart work
- ✓ Explain the importance of combining both
- ✓ Provide examples of how you have applied both approaches

15 How Quickly Do You Get Accustomed to New Technologies?

Interviewer Purpose: To assess the candidate's adaptability and technical skills

Applicant's Answer: I adapt quickly to new technologies due to my proactive learning approach I enjoy exploring new tools and systems, and I make an effort to stay updated with industry trends This adaptability has allowed me to integrate new technologies seamlessly into my work

- ✓ **Tips:**
- ✓ Highlight your proactive learning approach
- ✓ Provide examples of quickly adapting to new technologies
- ✓ Emphasize the importance of staying updated with industry trends

16 What Do You Enjoy Doing in Your Free Time?

Interviewer Purpose: To understand the candidate's interests outside of work and assess work-life balance
Applicant's Answer: In my free time, I enjoy activities that help me relax and recharge, such as reading, hiking, and volunteering These hobbies not only provide a break from work but also contribute to my personal growth and well-being

- ✓ **Tips:**
- ✓ Share your hobbies and interests
- ✓ Highlight how they contribute to personal growth
- ✓ Emphasize the importance of work-life balance

17 Would You Opt for a High-Paying Job You Don't Enjoy or a Lower-Paying Job You Are Passionate About?

Interviewer Purpose: To understand the candidate's priorities and values in their career

Applicant's Answer: I believe in finding a balance between financial stability and job satisfaction While a high-paying job is important, I would prefer a role that I am passionate about as it leads to greater long-term fulfillment and success Passion drives productivity and innovation, making it a key factor in my career choices

- ✓ **Tips:**
- ✓ Explain the importance of balancing financial stability and job satisfaction
- ✓ Highlight the benefits of working in a role you are passionate about
- ✓ Emphasize how passion drives productivity and success

18 In What Ways Do You Think Our Company Could Improve?

Interviewer Purpose: To gauge the candidate's understanding of the company and their ability to provide constructive feedback
Applicant's Answer: From my research, your company excels in many areas However, there might be opportunities to enhance customer engagement through more personalized services and leveraging advanced analytics for better decision-making I am excited about the prospect of contributing to these improvements

- ✓ **Tips:**
- ✓ Provide constructive feedback based on research
- ✓ Highlight specific areas for potential improvement
- ✓ Emphasize your enthusiasm to contribute to these improvements

5. Behaviorial Questions

1. Can You Describe a Situation Where You Had to Handle a Difficult Coworker and How You Managed It?

Interviewer Purpose: To evaluate your conflict resolution skills and teamwork abilities

Applicant's Answer: I once had a coworker whose working style was quite different from mine, leading to some friction To address this, I initiated a candid conversation to understand their perspective and shared my own We agreed on a few compromises, which improved our collaboration and ultimately enhanced our productivity as a team

- ✓ **Tips:**
- ✓ Focus on open communication
- ✓ Emphasize understanding different perspectives
- ✓ Highlight the positive outcome of resolving the conflict

2 Have You Ever Faced a Challenge in the Workplace? How Did You Handle It?

Interviewer Purpose: To understand your problem-solving skills and resilience in the face of challenges

Applicant's Answer: During a major project, our team faced unexpected technical issues that threatened our deadline I organized an emergency meeting, where we brainstormed and implemented a workaround solution By collaborating closely and putting in extra hours, we managed to deliver the project on time

- ✓ **Tips:**
- ✓ Describe the challenge clearly
- ✓ Highlight your proactive approach
- ✓ Emphasize the successful resolution and teamwork

3 Can You Share an Example of When You Performed Exceptionally Well Under Pressure?

Interviewer Purpose: To gauge your ability to perform under stressful conditions

Applicant's Answer: In my previous job, we had a tight deadline for a client presentation Despite the pressure, I maintained my focus and managed my time efficiently By prioritizing tasks and delegating where possible, I successfully completed the presentation, which impressed the client and secured a new contract

- ✓ **Tips:**
- ✓ Highlight your time management skills
- ✓ Emphasize staying calm and focused
- ✓ Share the positive outcome of handling pressure well

4 How Have You Demonstrated Leadership Qualities in the Past?

Interviewer Purpose: To assess your leadership skills and potential

Applicant's Answer: I led a cross-functional team on a complex project where effective coordination was crucial I facilitated regular meetings, set clear goals, and encouraged open communication By fostering a collaborative environment, we completed the project ahead of schedule and under budget

- ✓ **Tips:**
- ✓ Highlight your organizational skills
- ✓ Emphasize the importance of communication
- ✓ Share the successful outcome of your leadership

5 Describe a Time When You Had to Shift Your Priorities Quickly to Meet Changing Demands What Steps Did You Take?

Interviewer Purpose: To evaluate your adaptability and time management skills

Applicant's Answer: During a product launch, we received last-minute changes from the client I quickly reassessed the priorities, communicated the changes to the team, and adjusted our timeline By staying flexible and focused, we met the new requirements and successfully launched the product on time

- ✓ **Tips:**
- ✓ Highlight your adaptability
- ✓ Emphasize clear communication
- ✓ Share the successful outcome of meeting changing demands

6 Can You Talk About an Instance Where You Had to Deal With an Unhappy Customer? How Did You Address the Issue?

Interviewer Purpose: To understand your customer service skills and problem-solving abilities

Applicant's Answer: A customer was dissatisfied with a product issue I listened to their concerns, apologized for the inconvenience, and provided a solution by offering a replacement and a discount on their next purchase The customer appreciated the prompt resolution and continued to do business with us

- ✓ **Tips:**
- ✓ Emphasize active listening
- ✓ Highlight your problem-solving approach
- ✓ Share the positive outcome of resolving the issue

7 Can You Recall a Time When You Went Beyond Your Usual Responsibilities to Complete a Task?

Interviewer Purpose: To assess your dedication and willingness to take initiative

Applicant's Answer: During a critical project, our team was short-staffed I volunteered to take on additional responsibilities, working extra hours to ensure we met our deadlines My efforts were recognized, and we successfully delivered the project, earning praise from both the client and management

- ✓ **Tips:**
- ✓ Highlight your willingness to take initiative
- ✓ Emphasize your dedication to the team's success
- ✓ Share the positive recognition received for your efforts

8 Have You Ever Had to Make a Decision That Wasn't Popular? How Did You Deal With the Feedback?

Interviewer Purpose: To evaluate your decision-making skills and ability to handle criticism

Applicant's Answer: As a team leader, I once had to cut a beloved project feature due to budget constraints I communicated the reasoning transparently and focused on the project's overall success Although there was initial disappointment, my team understood and supported the decision as we delivered a successful final product

- ✓ **Tips:**
- ✓ Explain the rationale behind the decision
- ✓ Highlight the importance of transparent communication
- ✓ Emphasize handling feedback constructively

9 Can You Describe a Situation Where You Utilized Data or Analytics to Make a Decision? What Was the Result?

Interviewer Purpose: To assess your analytical skills and data-driven decision-making

Applicant's Answer: In a previous role, I used customer data to identify a declining trend in product satisfaction Analyzing the data, I pinpointed the issue and proposed a solution, which we implemented As a result, customer satisfaction improved by 20% within three months

- ✓ **Tips:**
- ✓ Describe the data analysis process
- ✓ Highlight your decision-making based on data
- ✓ Share the positive outcome of your data-driven decision

10 Share a Time When You Needed to Learn a New Skill to Finish a Task How Did You Go About It?

Interviewer Purpose: To understand your willingness to learn and adaptability

Applicant's Answer: For a project requiring advanced Excel skills, I realized I needed to upskill I took an online course and practiced extensively This new skill allowed me to complete the project efficiently and even train my colleagues, enhancing our team's overall productivity

- ✓ **Tips:**
- ✓ Highlight your proactive learning approach
- ✓ Emphasize the importance of continuous improvement
- ✓ Share the positive impact of acquiring the new skill

6. Teamwork Questions

1 How Would You Handle a Team Member Who Wasn't Contributing Their Fair Share of Work?

Interviewer Purpose: To understand your conflict resolution skills and ability to maintain team productivity

Applicant's Answer: If a team member wasn't contributing their fair share, I would first approach them privately to discuss the issue and understand any challenges they might be facing I would offer assistance and encourage open communication to find a solution If the situation didn't improve, I would involve the team leader to address the issue collectively

- ✓ **Tips:**
- ✓ Emphasize open communication
- ✓ Offer assistance and support
- ✓ Involve leadership if necessary

2 Can You Describe a Time When You Had to Work With Someone Whose Personality Clashed With Yours? How Did You Manage the Situation?

Interviewer Purpose: To assess your interpersonal skills and ability to work in diverse teams

Applicant's Answer: I once worked with a colleague who had a very different approach to problem-solving To manage this, I focused on finding common ground and fostering mutual respect We communicated openly about our differences and agreed on strategies that leveraged our individual strengths This collaboration improved our overall productivity

- ✓ **Tips:**
- ✓ Find common ground
- ✓ Foster mutual respect
- ✓ Leverage individual strengths

3 What Are the Three Key Qualities You Look for in a Teammate?

Interviewer Purpose: To understand your values and what you consider important in a collaborative work environment

Applicant's Answer: The three key qualities I value in a teammate are reliability, effective communication, and a positive attitude Reliability ensures that tasks are completed on time, effective communication fosters collaboration, and a positive attitude contributes to a supportive and productive work environment

- ✓ **Tips:**
- ✓ Highlight the importance of reliability
- ✓ Emphasize effective communication
- ✓ Mention the benefits of a positive attitude

4 How Do You Prefer to Work: Independently or as Part of a Team?

Interviewer Purpose: To determine your work style and how well you might fit into the team dynamic

Applicant's Answer: I enjoy both working independently and as part of a team Working independently allows me to focus and manage my time effectively, while teamwork offers opportunities for collaboration, idea sharing, and support I believe a balance between the two is crucial for achieving the best results

- ✓ **Tips:**
- ✓ Highlight the benefits of independent work
- ✓ Emphasize the value of teamwork
- ✓ Stress the importance of balance

5 How Would You Approach a Disagreement With a Team Member Regarding a Solution to a Problem?

Interviewer Purpose: To assess your problem-solving and collaboration skills

Applicant's Answer: In the event of a disagreement over a solution, I would first seek to understand my team member's perspective I would then present my viewpoint and work together to explore both options If necessary, we would seek input from other team members or a supervisor to reach a consensus that benefits the project

- ✓ **Tips:**
- ✓ Understand the other perspective
- ✓ Present your viewpoint clearly
- ✓ Seek consensus through collaboration

6 Can You Share an Instance When You Established a Professional Relationship With Someone You Initially Didn't Get Along With?

Interviewer Purpose: To evaluate your interpersonal skills and ability to build professional relationships

Applicant's Answer: I once had a colleague with whom I initially had little in common Over time, I made an effort to find common interests and engage in open conversations By focusing on our shared goals and working collaboratively, we built a strong professional relationship that enhanced our teamwork and productivity

- ✓ **Tips:**
- ✓ Find common interests
- ✓ Engage in open conversations
- ✓ Focus on shared goals

7 How Would Your Teammates Describe You?

Interviewer Purpose: To gain insight into your teamwork abilities and how you are perceived by others

Applicant's Answer: My teammates would likely describe me as reliable, collaborative, and positive They would highlight my dependability in meeting deadlines, my willingness to help others, and my ability to maintain a positive attitude even during challenging times

- ✓ **Tips:**
- ✓ Mention reliability
- ✓ Highlight collaborative spirit
- ✓ Emphasize a positive attitude

8 What Would Your Teammates Identify as Your Biggest Weakness?

Interviewer Purpose: To understand your self-awareness and willingness to improve

Applicant's Answer: My teammates might say that I sometimes take on too much responsibility, trying to handle everything myself However, I've been working on delegating tasks more effectively and trusting my team members to share the workload, which has improved our overall efficiency

- ✓ **Tips:**
- ✓ Acknowledge the weakness
- ✓ Highlight steps taken to improve
- ✓ Emphasize the positive outcome of these efforts

9 Can You Give an Example of When You Worked Together With Your Team to Complete a Critical Project or Meet a Tight Deadline?

Interviewer Purpose: To evaluate your teamwork and project management skills

Applicant's Answer: In my previous role, our team had to meet a tight deadline for a major project We divided the tasks based on each member's strengths and maintained open communication throughout the process By collaborating effectively and supporting each other, we successfully completed the project ahead of schedule

Tips:

- ✓ Highlight task delegation
- ✓ Emphasize open communication
- ✓ Mention the successful completion

10 Do You Prefer Taking on a Leadership Role or Following Instructions?

Interviewer Purpose: To understand your preferred work style and leadership potential

Applicant's Answer: I am comfortable in both roles I enjoy taking on leadership responsibilities, where I can guide and motivate the team However, I also recognize the importance of following instructions and supporting others Flexibility in switching between these roles is key to the success of any project

- ✓ **Tips:**
- ✓ Highlight your comfort in both roles
- ✓ Emphasize the importance of flexibility
- ✓ Mention the benefits of adapting to the situation

11 How Do You Go About Delegating Tasks to Members of Your Team?

Interviewer Purpose: To understand your approach to task delegation and management

Applicant's Answer: I delegate tasks by first assessing each team member's strengths and skillsets I then assign tasks based on these strengths and provide clear instructions and expectations I ensure regular check-ins to monitor progress and offer support as needed, making adjustments if necessary to align with team goals

- ✓ **Tips:** Assess team members' strengths
- ✓ Provide clear instructions and expectations
- ✓ Monitor progress with regular check-ins

12 How Would You Foster Respect Within Your Team?

Interviewer Purpose: To evaluate your strategies for building a respectful and cohesive team environment

Applicant's Answer: To promote respect, I model respectful behavior and encourage open communication I ensure that everyone's opinions are valued and address any conflicts or issues promptly Regular team meetings and feedback sessions help reinforce a culture of mutual respect and collaboration

- ✓ **Tips:** Model respectful behavior
- ✓ Encourage open communication
- ✓ Address conflicts promptly

13 What Techniques Do You Use to Motivate Your Team?

Interviewer Purpose: To assess your methods for keeping team members engaged and motivated

Applicant's Answer: I motivate my team by setting clear and achievable goals, recognizing and rewarding their achievements, and providing opportunities for professional growth I also make an effort to understand each team member's individual motivators and tailor my approach accordingly.

- ✓ **Tips:** Set clear and achievable goals
- ✓ Recognize and reward achievements
- ✓ Provide opportunities for professional growth

14 What Team-Building Activities Do You Think Would Benefit This Team?

Interviewer Purpose: To gauge your ideas for enhancing team cohesion and collaboration

Applicant's Answer: Team-building activities such as collaborative problem-solving exercises, workshops, and social events can greatly benefit the team These activities encourage communication, strengthen relationships, and build trust among team members, contributing to a more cohesive and effective team

- ✓ **Tips:**
- ✓ Incorporate collaborative exercises
- ✓ Organize workshops and social events
- ✓ Focus on activities that build trust and communication

15 If Your Team Were Facing Budget Cuts and You Had to Lay Off Two Employees, How Would You Make That Decision?

Interviewer Purpose: To understand your decision-making process in difficult situations

Applicant's Answer: In such a scenario, I would evaluate each employee's performance, skills, and contribution to the team I would consider factors such as their impact on the project and the overall team dynamic I would also consult with HR and consider legal and ethical implications before making a final decision

- ✓ **Tips:**
- ✓ Evaluate performance and skills
- ✓ Consider impact on the team
- ✓ Consult with HR and consider implications.

7. Dependable or Reliable Questions

1 How Do You Ensure Accountability in Your Daily Work Routine?

Interviewer Purpose: To assess your reliability and self-management skills
Applicant's Answer: I ensure accountability by setting clear daily goals and regularly reviewing my progress I prioritize my tasks based on urgency and importance, and I make use of tools like to-do lists and project management software to stay organized By maintaining open communication with my team, I keep everyone informed about my progress and any potential roadblocks

- ✓ **Tips:**
- ✓ Set clear daily goals
- ✓ Use organizational tools
- ✓ Maintain open communication

2 Describe the Methods and Tools You Use to Keep Yourself Organized and Accountable at Work

Interviewer Purpose: To understand how you maintain organization and accountability
Applicant's Answer: I rely on several tools to stay organized, such as task management apps, calendars, and spreadsheets I also follow a structured routine, breaking down larger projects into manageable tasks and setting deadlines for each Regular check-ins with my team help me stay on track and ensure accountability

- ✓ **Tips:**
- ✓ Utilize task management tools
- ✓ Break projects into manageable tasks
- ✓ Conduct regular check-ins

3 How Do You Handle Multiple Tasks Simultaneously?

Interviewer Purpose: To evaluate your multitasking and prioritization skills

Applicant's Answer: When managing multiple tasks, I prioritize them based on deadlines and importance I use a task management tool to track my progress and ensure I stay on top of everything Additionally, I allocate specific time blocks for each task, minimizing distractions to maintain focus and efficiency

- ✓ **Tips:**
- ✓ Prioritize tasks by deadline and importance
- ✓ Use task management tools
- ✓ Allocate specific time blocks for tasks

4 Explain Your Approach to Managing Your Time and Prioritizing Tasks Each Day

Interviewer Purpose: To understand your time management and prioritization strategies

Applicant's Answer: I start each day by reviewing my task list and identifying the most urgent and important tasks I then create a schedule that allocates time for each task, ensuring that I stay focused and productive By regularly reassessing my priorities, I can adapt to any changes or urgent needs that arise

- ✓ **Tips:**
- ✓ Review and prioritize your task list
- ✓ Create a daily schedule
- ✓ Reassess priorities regularly

5 Can You Share a Time When You Found It Challenging to Meet a Deadline? How Did You Handle It?

Interviewer Purpose: To gauge your problem-solving and time management skills under pressure
Applicant's Answer: There was a project with an unexpectedly tight deadline due to last-minute changes I tackled this by working extra hours and seeking help from my colleagues to divide the workload We communicated frequently to ensure everything stayed on track, and ultimately, we completed the project on time

- ✓ **Tips:**
- ✓ Work extra hours if necessary
- ✓ Seek help from colleagues
- ✓ Maintain frequent communication

6 How Do You Stay on Track and Maintain Productivity Without Supervision?

Interviewer Purpose: To assess your ability to work independently and remain productive
Applicant's Answer: Without supervision, I rely on self-discipline and a structured routine to stay productive I set clear goals and deadlines for myself and use productivity tools to track my progress Regular self-assessments help me identify any areas where I need to improve or adjust my approach

- ✓ **Tips:**
- ✓ Maintain a structured routine
- ✓ Set clear goals and deadlines
- ✓ Conduct regular self-assessments

7 If a Colleague Is Lagging Behind in Their Work and It Threatens the Team's Deadline, but You're on Schedule, What Would You Do?

Interviewer Purpose: To understand your teamwork and problem-solving approach in collaborative settings
Applicant's Answer: If a colleague is falling behind, I would first offer my assistance to help them catch up I would also communicate with the team to reallocate tasks if necessary, ensuring that we stay on track to meet the deadline Collaboration and open communication are key to resolving such situations

- ✓ **Tips:**
- ✓ Offer assistance to colleagues
- ✓ Reallocate tasks if needed
- ✓ Maintain open communication

8. Decision making Questions

1 Can You Describe a Situation Where You Had to Make Adjustments Due to Factors Beyond Your Control? How Did You Handle It?

Interviewer Purpose: To assess your ability to adapt to unforeseen circumstances and maintain productivity

Applicant's Answer: During a major project, a key stakeholder's requirements changed unexpectedly I immediately reassessed the project plan and communicated the changes to my team We adjusted our timeline and redistributed tasks to meet the new requirements By staying flexible and maintaining open communication, we successfully adapted and completed the project on time

- ✓ **Tips:**
- ✓ Reassess and adjust plans quickly
- ✓ Communicate changes clearly
- ✓ Stay flexible and proactive

2 How Do You Cope With Frequently Changing Deadlines?

Interviewer Purpose: To evaluate your ability to manage time and prioritize tasks under shifting conditions

Applicant's Answer: I cope with changing deadlines by maintaining a dynamic task list and regularly reassessing my priorities I stay in close contact with my team and stakeholders to keep everyone informed of any changes This allows me to reallocate resources and adjust my schedule to ensure that critical tasks are completed on time

- ✓ **Tips:**
- ✓ Maintain a dynamic task list
- ✓ Reassess priorities regularly
- ✓ Communicate changes effectively

3 When Was the Last Time You Dealt With a Last-Minute Request? What Actions Did You Take?

Interviewer Purpose: To understand your problem-solving skills and ability to handle unexpected tasks

Applicant's Answer: Recently, I received a last-minute request to prepare a presentation for an urgent client meeting I quickly gathered the necessary information and prioritized the task By focusing solely on this request and utilizing my existing knowledge and resources, I was able to complete the presentation on time and to a high standard

- ✓ **Tips:**
- ✓ Prioritize the urgent task
- ✓ Utilize existing resources
- ✓ Focus on the task at hand

4 How Do You Balance Multiple Important Projects Competing for Your Time and Energy?

Interviewer Purpose: To assess your multitasking and time management skills

Applicant's Answer: When faced with multiple important projects, I prioritize based on deadlines and impact I create a detailed schedule that allocates time blocks for each project and ensure regular progress reviews This structured approach allows me to manage my time effectively and ensure that each project receives the necessary attention

- ✓ **Tips:**
- ✓ Prioritize based on deadlines and impact
- ✓ Create a detailed schedule
- ✓ Conduct regular progress reviews

5 What Significant Adjustments Have You Made in Your Career?

Interviewer Purpose: To gauge your adaptability and willingness to embrace change

Applicant's Answer: A significant adjustment I made in my career was transitioning from a technical role to a managerial position This required me to develop new skills in leadership, communication, and project management I took additional training courses and sought mentorship to successfully navigate this transition and excel in my new role

- ✓ **Tips:**
- ✓ Develop new skills relevant to the change
- ✓ Seek additional training
- ✓ Find a mentor for guidance

6 Explain a Scenario Where You Had to Quickly Make a Decision Under Pressure How Did You Approach It?

Interviewer Purpose: To evaluate your decision-making skills and ability to perform under pressure

Applicant's Answer: During a product launch, a critical issue arose that threatened our timeline I quickly gathered the team to assess the problem and brainstorm solutions After evaluating the options, I made a decisive choice to implement the most viable solution This swift action allowed us to address the issue and launch the product successfully

- ✓ **Tips:**
- ✓ Assess the problem quickly
- ✓ Brainstorm and evaluate solutions
- ✓ Make a decisive choice and act promptly

7 Describe Your Daily Work Routine How Do You Manage Unexpected Challenges?

Interviewer Purpose: To understand your organizational skills and adaptability to unforeseen events

Applicant's Answer: My daily work routine involves reviewing my task list and setting priorities I allocate specific time blocks for each task and maintain flexibility to accommodate unexpected challenges When surprises arise, I reassess my priorities and adjust my schedule to ensure that urgent issues are addressed without compromising overall productivity

- ✓ **Tips:**
- ✓ Review and prioritize tasks daily
- ✓ Allocate specific time blocks
- ✓ Maintain flexibility for unexpected challenges

8 Share an Instance When You Needed Additional Training or Guidance to Complete a Task What Steps Did You Take?

Interviewer Purpose: To gauge your willingness to seek help and learn new skills

Applicant's Answer: When I was assigned a task requiring advanced data analysis, I realized I needed additional training I enrolled in an online course to develop the necessary skills and sought guidance from colleagues with expertise in the area By proactively seeking help and dedicating time to learn, I successfully completed the task and improved my overall skill set

- ✓ **Tips:**
- ✓ Identify the need for additional skills
- ✓ Enroll in relevant training
- ✓ Seek guidance from knowledgeable colleagues

9. Leadership Questions

1 How Do You Approach Setting a Vision for Your Team or Organization?

Interviewer Purpose: To understand your ability to establish a clear direction and inspire others

Applicant's Answer: Setting a vision involves understanding both the current landscape and future opportunities I start by analyzing trends and gathering input from key stakeholders I then articulate a clear, compelling vision that aligns with organizational goals By communicating this vision effectively, I aim to inspire and align my team towards achieving our shared objectives

- ✓ **Tips:**
- ✓ Analyze trends and gather input
- ✓ Articulate a clear and compelling vision
- ✓ Communicate effectively to inspire and align

2 Describe a Situation Where You Had to Lead Through a Crisis What Strategies Did You Use?

Interviewer Purpose: To evaluate your crisis management and leadership under pressure

Applicant's Answer: During a significant system outage, I took charge by first assessing the situation and prioritizing immediate actions I communicated transparently with the team and stakeholders about the steps we were taking and delegated tasks based on urgency My focus was on quick resolution, maintaining morale, and reviewing our response to improve future crisis management

- ✓ **Tips:**
- ✓ Assess the situation and prioritize actions
- ✓ Communicate transparently with all stakeholders
- ✓ Focus on quick resolution and future improvements

3 Can You Provide an Example of How You've Mentored or Developed Others in Your Career?

Interviewer Purpose: To gauge your ability to support and develop others' skills and careers
Applicant's Answer: I have mentored several colleagues by providing regular feedback, setting developmental goals, and offering guidance on their career path For example, I helped a junior team member improve their presentation skills through constructive feedback and practice sessions, which ultimately led to their successful promotion

- ✓ **Tips:**
- ✓ Provide regular, constructive feedback
- ✓ Set clear developmental goals
- ✓ Offer practical guidance and support

4 How Do You Handle Making Difficult Decisions That May Not Be Popular?

Interviewer Purpose: To assess your decision-making process and ability to handle unpopular choices
Applicant's Answer: When making difficult decisions, I consider all available data and perspectives before reaching a conclusion I communicate the rationale behind the decision transparently to ensure understanding, even if the outcome is unpopular My focus is on the long-term benefits and maintaining fairness and integrity throughout the process
Tips:

1. Evaluate all data and perspectives
2. Communicate the rationale transparently
3. Focus on long-term benefits and fairness

5 What Methods Do You Use to Foster Innovation Within Your Organization?

Interviewer Purpose: To understand your approach to encouraging creative thinking and innovation
Applicant's Answer: To foster innovation, I create an environment that encourages experimentation and risk-taking I promote brainstorming sessions, provide resources for new projects, and support a culture where creative ideas are valued and explored Regularly celebrating innovative successes and learning from failures helps to maintain a dynamic and forward-thinking atmosphere

- ✓ **Tips:**
- ✓ Encourage experimentation and risk-taking
- ✓ Provide resources and support for new projects
- ✓ Celebrate successes and learn from failures

6 Describe a Time When You Had to Influence Others to Embrace a New Strategy or Change

Interviewer Purpose: To assess your ability to lead and influence others through change
Applicant's Answer: I once led a shift to a new project management system that initially faced resistance I addressed concerns by organizing demonstrations, explaining the benefits, and involving key stakeholders in the transition process By showing the positive impact and providing support, I successfully gained buy-in and facilitated a smooth transition
Tips:

1. Address concerns through demonstrations and explanations
2. Involve key stakeholders in the process
3. Show the positive impact and provide support

7 How Do You Balance Long-Term Vision with Short-Term Goals in Your Leadership Role?

Interviewer Purpose: To understand how you manage and integrate strategic and operational objectives
Applicant's Answer: Balancing long-term vision with short-term goals involves aligning immediate tasks with overarching objectives I set clear, measurable short-term goals that contribute to the long-term vision and regularly review progress to ensure alignment This approach helps maintain focus on strategic priorities while achieving necessary short-term outcomes

- ✓ **Tips:**
- ✓ Align short-term goals with long-term vision
- ✓ Set measurable objectives
- ✓ Regularly review progress for alignment

8 Can You Share an Example of How You've Encouraged Accountability in Your Leadership?

Interviewer Purpose: To gauge your ability to promote responsibility and accountability within your team

Applicant's Answer: I encourage accountability by setting clear expectations and creating a culture of ownership For instance, in a previous role, I implemented regular check-ins and performance reviews, ensuring that each team member understood their responsibilities and how their work contributed to the team's success This approach led to improved performance and accountability

Tips:

1. Set clear expectations
2. Create a culture of ownership
3. Conduct regular check-ins and reviews

9 How Do You Manage Conflict Between Team Members or Departments?

Interviewer Purpose: To evaluate your conflict resolution skills and ability to maintain a harmonious work environment

Applicant's Answer: I manage conflict by addressing issues early and facilitating open discussions between the parties involved I focus on understanding each perspective and finding common ground By mediating the conversation and guiding towards a mutually agreeable solution, I help resolve conflicts effectively and maintain a positive work environment

- ✓ **Tips:**
- ✓ Address conflicts early
- ✓ Facilitate open discussions
- ✓ Find common ground and guide towards a solution

10 How Do You Ensure That Your Leadership Style Adapts to Different Situations and Individuals?

Interviewer Purpose: To understand your flexibility and ability to tailor your leadership approach

Applicant's Answer: I adapt my leadership style by assessing the needs of the situation and the individuals involved I consider factors such as team dynamics, project requirements, and personal preferences By being flexible and responsive, I can adjust my approach to effectively lead in various contexts and support diverse team members

Tips:

1. Assess the needs of the situation and individuals
2. Be flexible and responsive
3. Adjust your approach to suit different contexts

10. Problem Solving Questions

1 Describe a Situation Where You Took Initiative to Identify and Resolve a Problem

Interviewer Purpose: To assess your proactive problem-solving skills
Applicant's Answer: In a previous role, I noticed a recurring issue with data entry errors I took the initiative to investigate and discovered that the problem was due to outdated software I proposed and implemented an upgrade, which significantly reduced errors and improved overall efficiency

- ✓ **Tips:**
- ✓ Identify recurring issues early
- ✓ Investigate the root cause
- ✓ Propose and implement practical solutions

2 How Do You Address Mistakes or Inaccuracies in Your Own Work?

Interviewer Purpose: To understand your approach to self-correction and accountability
Applicant's Answer: When I find a mistake in my work, I first acknowledge and assess the error to understand its impact I then correct the mistake promptly and take steps to prevent it from recurring, such as revising my processes or seeking feedback to improve accuracy

- ✓ **Tips:**
- ✓ Acknowledge the error quickly
- ✓ Assess and correct the mistake promptly
- ✓ Implement measures to prevent recurrence

3 What Approach Do You Take to Evaluate the Advantages and Disadvantages of a Decision?

Interviewer Purpose: To evaluate your decision-making process
Applicant's Answer: I use a structured approach to weigh the pros and cons of a decision by listing potential benefits and drawbacks I consider the impact on all stakeholders and use this analysis to make

an informed choice This helps ensure that the decision aligns with both short-term needs and long-term goals

- ✓ **Tips:**
- ✓ List and analyze potential benefits and drawbacks
- ✓ Consider the impact on stakeholders
- ✓ Align decisions with long-term goals

4 What Actions Do You Take When There's No Established System for Resolving a Problem?

Interviewer Purpose: To gauge your problem-solving creativity and resourcefulness
Applicant's Answer: In the absence of a set system, I start by researching best practices and similar solutions I then consult with colleagues or experts to gather insights Based on this information, I develop a customized solution, test it, and refine it as needed to address the issue effectively

- ✓ **Tips:**
- ✓ Research best practices and similar solutions
- ✓ Seek insights from colleagues or experts
- ✓ Develop and test a customized solution

5 What Steps Do You Follow in Your Problem-Solving Process?

Interviewer Purpose: To understand your systematic approach to solving problems
Applicant's Answer: My problem-solving process involves identifying the problem, gathering relevant information, generating potential solutions, evaluating these solutions, and then implementing the best option I follow up to ensure the problem is resolved and make adjustments if necessary

- ✓ **Tips:**
- ✓ Identify the problem clearly
- ✓ Generate and evaluate potential solutions
- ✓ Implement and review the chosen solution

6 What Resources Do You Utilize to Solve Problems?

Interviewer Purpose: To assess the resources and tools you rely on for problem-solving

Applicant's Answer: I use a variety of resources to solve problems, including online research, industry reports, and professional networks I also leverage internal data and tools, and seek advice from colleagues with relevant expertise to ensure a comprehensive approach to problem-solving

- ✓ **Tips:**
- ✓ Use online research and industry reports
- ✓ Leverage internal data and tools
- ✓ Seek advice from knowledgeable colleagues

7 How Would You Deal With a "This Is How We've Always Done It" Mindset on Your Team?

Interviewer Purpose: To evaluate your approach to overcoming resistance to change

Applicant's Answer: I would address this mindset by presenting evidence of potential improvements and benefits from changing the current approach I would involve the team in discussions, gather feedback, and propose a trial period for the new method to demonstrate its advantages

- ✓ **Tips:**
- ✓ Present evidence of potential benefits
- ✓ Involve the team in discussions and feedback
- ✓ Propose a trial period to test new methods

8 Can You Describe the Most Recent Problem You Solved and Its Outcome?

Interviewer Purpose: To get a recent example of your problem-solving abilities and their effectiveness

Applicant's Answer: Recently, I dealt with a sudden drop in customer satisfaction I investigated the root causes by analyzing feedback and service metrics I implemented new training for the customer service team and revised our support processes, which resulted in a significant improvement in customer satisfaction scores

- ✓ **Tips:**

- ✓ Analyze feedback and metrics
- ✓ Implement targeted solutions
- ✓ Measure the impact and adjust as needed

9 What Has Been the Most Significant Challenge You've Overcome in Your Career?

Interviewer Purpose: To understand your resilience and problem-solving capabilities
Applicant's Answer: One major challenge I faced was leading a project with tight deadlines and limited resources I prioritized tasks, optimized workflows, and communicated effectively with the team Despite the constraints, we completed the project on time and within budget, which was a significant achievement

- ✓ **Tips:**
- ✓ Prioritize tasks and optimize workflows
- ✓ Communicate effectively with the team
- ✓ Focus on meeting deadlines and budget constraints

10 How Would You Approach a Task That Is New to You and Outside Your Comfort Zone?

Interviewer Purpose: To assess your willingness to tackle unfamiliar challenges and your learning approach
Applicant's Answer: When faced with a new task, I start by conducting thorough research and seeking guidance from experienced colleagues I also break the task into smaller, manageable steps and set milestones to track progress This approach helps me build confidence and ensure successful completion

- ✓ **Tips:**
- ✓ Conduct research and seek guidance
- ✓ Break the task into manageable steps
- ✓ Set milestones to track progress

11. Research Questions

1 How Do You Handle Situations When Reliable Sources Are Not Available?

Interviewer Purpose: To evaluate your problem-solving approach when facing a lack of reliable information
Applicant's Answer: When reliable sources are unavailable, I first seek alternative sources or consult industry experts I also use my professional network to gather insights If necessary, I rely on my own analysis and experience to make informed decisions while clearly noting the limitations of the available information
Tips:

- ✓ Seek alternative sources and consult experts
- ✓ Use your professional network for additional insights
- ✓ Clearly note any limitations in the information used

2 How Do You Ensure That Sources You Use Are Properly Cited and Utilized in Your Work?

Interviewer Purpose: To assess your adherence to proper citation practices and effective use of sources
Applicant's Answer: I ensure sources are properly cited by following relevant citation guidelines and keeping detailed records of all references I use these sources to support my work by integrating the information accurately into my analysis or reports and providing proper attribution to avoid plagiarism
Tips:

- ✓ Follow citation guidelines and keep detailed records
- ✓ Integrate information accurately into your work
- ✓ Provide proper attribution to avoid plagiarism

3 Describe a Recent Instance Where Research Helped You Resolve a Problem

Interviewer Purpose: To understand how you apply research to practical problem-solving
Applicant's Answer: Recently, I faced a challenge with a project's declining performance metrics I conducted research on industry

trends and similar case studies, which led me to implement new strategies that addressed the performance issues The outcome was a significant improvement in metrics and overall project success

- ✓ **Tips:**
- ✓ Conduct thorough research on relevant trends
- ✓ Apply insights to address specific challenges
- ✓ Evaluate the impact of your solutions on the problem

4 Explain How You Use Research to Justify Your Opinions to Colleagues and Clients

Interviewer Purpose: To gauge how effectively you use research to support your arguments
Applicant's Answer: I use research to support my opinions by presenting data and evidence in a clear and structured manner I provide relevant examples and case studies to back up my points, and I ensure that my sources are credible This approach helps in persuading colleagues and clients by demonstrating a well-researched basis for my views

- ✓ **Tips:**
- ✓ Present data and evidence clearly
- ✓ Use relevant examples and case studies
- ✓ Ensure sources are credible to support your points

5 What Criteria Do You Use to Determine the Reliability of a Source?

Interviewer Purpose: To assess your ability to evaluate the credibility of information sources
Applicant's Answer: I determine the reliability of a source by checking its credibility, such as the author's qualifications, publication reputation, and the source's currency I also look for corroboration from other reputable sources to confirm the accuracy of the information

- ✓ **Tips:**
- ✓ Check the author's qualifications and publication reputation
- ✓ Ensure the source is current and relevant

- ✓ Look for corroboration from other reputable sources

6 How Do You Manage Conflicting Information from Different Resources?

Interviewer Purpose: To understand how you resolve discrepancies in information
Applicant's Answer: When faced with conflicting information, I analyze each source's context and credibility I seek additional sources to verify facts and look for common ground I also consult with experts if necessary to clarify ambiguities and make informed decisions based on the most reliable information available

- ✓ **Tips:** Analyze context and credibility of each source
- ✓ Seek additional sources for verification
- ✓ Consult experts to clarify ambiguities

7 What Is Your Approach to Using Industry Resources in Your Work?

Interviewer Purpose: To understand how you incorporate industry-specific resources into your work
Applicant's Answer: I integrate industry resources into my work by regularly reviewing relevant publications, reports, and data I use these resources to stay updated on trends and best practices, which helps in making informed decisions and enhancing the quality of my work

- ✓ **Tips:**
- ✓ Regularly review relevant industry publications and reports
- ✓ Use resources to stay updated on trends and best practices
- ✓ Apply insights to enhance decision-making and work quality

8. **What Makes a Source Reliable in Your Opinion?**
Interviewer Purpose: To gauge your criteria for evaluating the trustworthiness of sources
Applicant's Answer: A reliable source is typically authored by an expert in the field, published by a reputable organization, and supported by evidence or data Additionally, it should be recent and relevant to the topic at hand to ensure the information is accurate and applicable

- ✓ **Tips:**
- ✓ Check for expertise and reputable publication
- ✓ Ensure the source is supported by evidence
- ✓ Verify the information is recent and relevant

9 How Do You Incorporate Sources into Your Work to Enhance Your Arguments?

Interviewer Purpose: To assess how effectively you integrate sources to support your arguments
Applicant's Answer: I incorporate sources by directly linking their findings to the points I'm making I provide citations and contextualize the information within my work, ensuring that the source's credibility supports my argument This approach helps build a strong, evidence-based case

- ✓ **Tips:**
- ✓ Link source findings directly to your points
- ✓ Provide clear citations and context
- ✓ Use credible sources to strengthen your argument

10 What Is Your Method for Using Research to Inform Your Decisions?

Interviewer Purpose: To understand your process for applying research findings to decision-making
Applicant's Answer: My method involves gathering relevant research, analyzing the data, and applying it to the decision-making process I weigh the research findings against current objectives and constraints, ensuring that decisions are informed by solid evidence and aligned with overall goals

- ✓ **Tips:** Gather and analyze relevant research data
- ✓ Apply findings to decision-making process

12. Creativity Questions

1 Can You Share an Example of a Company That Successfully Used Creativity to Address a Challenge?

Interviewer Purpose: To gauge your awareness of creative problem-solving in different organizations

Applicant's Answer: One example is how Netflix used creativity to pivot from DVD rentals to a streaming service model They recognized early on that the future of media consumption was digital and acted on that insight by developing a user-friendly streaming platform, which transformed their business and the industry

- ✓ **Tips:**
- ✓ Look for innovative solutions that transformed industry practices
- ✓ Identify key decisions that drove the success of creative strategies
- ✓ Understand the impact of creative thinking on business models

2 Describe a Situation Where You Applied Creative Thinking to Resolve a Problem

Interviewer Purpose: To understand how you personally apply creativity to problem-solving
Applicant's Answer: In my previous role, I faced a challenge with declining engagement in our marketing campaigns I proposed using interactive content and gamification to engage users more effectively This creative approach increased user interaction by 40% and significantly improved campaign performance

- ✓ **Tips:**
- ✓ Highlight specific creative solutions you've implemented
- ✓ Provide measurable outcomes to demonstrate effectiveness
- ✓ Show how your approach addressed the core problem

3 How Would You Incorporate Creativity into This Role?

Interviewer Purpose: To assess your ability to apply creative thinking in the new position
Applicant's Answer: In this role, I would use creativity to develop innovative solutions to enhance project outcomes For instance, I would propose brainstorming sessions and encourage team members to explore unconventional approaches to problem-solving, aiming to improve processes and deliver better results

- ✓ **Tips:**
- ✓ Suggest practical ways to apply creativity in the role
- ✓ Emphasize methods to foster innovative thinking
- ✓ Connect creative approaches to achieving role objectives

4 What Strategies Do You Use to Encourage Creativity in Your Work?

Interviewer Purpose: To evaluate your methods for fostering creativity in your professional environment
Applicant's Answer: I promote creativity by creating an open environment where team members feel comfortable sharing ideas I encourage regular brainstorming sessions and provide time and resources for experimentation Recognizing and rewarding innovative contributions also helps motivate creativity

- ✓ **Tips:**
- ✓ Create an open and supportive environment for idea-sharing
- ✓ Schedule regular brainstorming sessions
- ✓ Recognize and reward creative contributions

5 How Do You Foster Creativity Among Your Team Members?

Interviewer Purpose: To understand how you inspire creativity within a team setting
Applicant's Answer: I foster team creativity by encouraging diverse viewpoints and facilitating collaborative brainstorming I also provide opportunities for team members to take ownership of projects and experiment with new ideas This approach helps cultivate a culture of innovation and collective problem-solving

- ✓ **Tips:**
- ✓ Encourage diverse viewpoints and collaboration
- ✓ Provide opportunities for ownership and experimentation
- ✓ Cultivate a culture that values innovation and creativity

6 How Do You React to Innovative Ideas That Are Unconventional But Persuasive?

Interviewer Purpose: To assess your openness to unconventional yet compelling ideas

Applicant's Answer: I welcome innovative ideas, even if they are unconventional, as long as they are well-supported by evidence I evaluate their potential impact and feasibility, and if they align with our goals, I'm open to piloting them to explore their effectiveness

- ✓ **Tips:**
- ✓ Evaluate the potential impact and feasibility of ideas
- ✓ Be open to piloting unconventional concepts
- ✓ Ensure alignment with overall goals and objectives

7 What Is the Most Creative Project or Idea You've Developed in Your Current Role?

Interviewer Purpose: To highlight your ability to generate and implement creative ideas

Applicant's Answer: One of my most creative projects involved redesigning our customer feedback system to include gamification elements This approach increased user participation and provided more actionable insights The project not only enhanced our feedback mechanism but also engaged users more effectively

Tips:

- ✓ Describe a specific project or idea and its impact
- ✓ Highlight how creativity was applied
- ✓ Focus on measurable improvements and outcomes

8 Do You Prefer Experimenting with New Processes or Maintaining Existing Effective Ones?

Interviewer Purpose: To determine your attitude toward experimentation versus maintaining established processes

Applicant's Answer: I believe in a balanced approach While I value maintaining effective processes, I also see the benefit of experimenting with new methods to drive innovation I assess the potential benefits of new approaches and implement them when they align with our goals and improve efficiency

- ✓ **Tips:** Balance experimentation with maintaining effective processes
- ✓ Evaluate the potential benefits of new approaches
- ✓ Ensure alignment with goals and efficiency improvements

9 What Was the Last New Idea You Implemented at Work?

Interviewer Purpose: To understand your recent experiences with innovation
Applicant's Answer: The last new idea I implemented was a revised approach to our onboarding process, incorporating interactive digital tools and personalized training modules This change improved new hire engagement and reduced the time to productivity, leading to a smoother onboarding experience

- ✓ **Tips:** Provide details of the idea and its implementation
- ✓ Focus on the outcomes and improvements achieved
- ✓ Highlight how the idea addressed a specific need or challenge

10 How Do You Approach Using Creativity in Problem Solving?

Interviewer Purpose: To assess your methodology for applying creative thinking to solve problems
Applicant's Answer: I approach creative problem-solving by first clearly defining the problem and then exploring a range of potential solutions I encourage brainstorming sessions, leverage diverse perspectives, and test different approaches to find the most effective resolution

- ✓ **Tips:** Clearly define the problem before brainstorming
- ✓ Encourage diverse perspectives and ideas
- ✓ Test and evaluate different approaches to find the best solution.

13. Integrity Questions

1 What Does Integrity Mean to You?

Interviewer Purpose: To understand your personal definition of integrity and how it influences your actions

Applicant's Answer: To me, integrity means consistently adhering to moral and ethical principles, even when no one is watching It involves being honest, transparent, and accountable in all actions and decisions Integrity is about doing the right thing, even if it's challenging or inconvenient

- ✓ **Tips:**
- ✓ Define integrity clearly and concisely
- ✓ Relate it to personal and professional behavior
- ✓ Highlight the importance of honesty and accountability

2 How Do You Show Respect in the Workplace?

Interviewer Purpose: To gauge how you demonstrate respect and foster a positive work environment
Applicant's Answer: I show respect in the workplace by actively listening to others, valuing diverse perspectives, and treating everyone with kindness and fairness I make an effort to communicate clearly and supportively, acknowledging the contributions of my colleagues and addressing any concerns with empathy

- ✓ **Tips:**
- ✓ Emphasize active listening and valuing diverse perspectives
- ✓ Demonstrate kindness and fairness in interactions
- ✓ Address concerns with empathy and respect

3 What Would You Do If You Discovered a Team Member Violating Company Policies?

Interviewer Purpose: To assess your approach to handling breaches of company rules
Applicant's Answer: If I found a team member breaking company rules, I would first approach the situation with a focus on understanding the context I would discuss the issue privately with the individual to address the

behavior and remind them of the company's policies If necessary, I would escalate the matter to the appropriate channels to ensure it is resolved in accordance with company guidelines

- ✓ **Tips:**
- ✓ Approach the situation privately and factually
- ✓ Address the behavior while reminding them of company policies
- ✓ Escalate to appropriate channels if needed

4 How Would You Handle Discovering a Manager Breaking Company Rules?

Interviewer Purpose: To evaluate how you would address ethical issues involving higher-level staff
Applicant's Answer: If I found a manager breaking company rules, I would first document the behavior and seek to understand the context I would then consider discussing the issue with the manager directly, depending on the severity If the behavior continues or is significant, I would escalate the issue to a higher authority or use formal reporting mechanisms to address it

- ✓ **Tips:**
- ✓ Document the behavior and understand the context
- ✓ Consider direct discussion with the manager, if appropriate
- ✓ Use formal reporting mechanisms if necessary

5 Can You Share a Time When Your Integrity Was Tested?

Interviewer Purpose: To gain insight into your personal experience with maintaining integrity under challenging circumstances
Applicant's Answer: Once, I was offered a bonus for completing a project faster, but the offer involved cutting corners that would compromise quality I chose to decline the offer and completed the project to the best of my ability, adhering to all standards This decision reinforced my commitment to maintaining integrity, even under pressure

- ✓ **Tips:**
- ✓ Describe the challenge and your decision-making process
- ✓ Highlight the importance of upholding standards
- ✓ Reflect on how the experience reinforced your values

6 How Do You Handle Making Mistakes at Work?

Interviewer Purpose: To understand your approach to addressing and correcting errors
Applicant's Answer: When I make a mistake, I take immediate responsibility and assess what went wrong I inform relevant parties, correct the error as quickly as possible, and analyze how to prevent similar issues in the future I also seek feedback to improve my processes and learn from the experience

- ✓ **Tips:**
- ✓ Take responsibility and address the mistake promptly
- ✓ Implement corrective measures and prevention strategies
- ✓ Seek feedback and learn from the experience

7 How Do You Maintain Confidentiality in the Workplace?

Interviewer Purpose: To evaluate your practices for handling sensitive information
Applicant's Answer: I maintain confidentiality by adhering to company policies regarding sensitive information I ensure that confidential data is only accessed by authorized personnel and use secure methods for handling and storing such information I am also vigilant about not discussing confidential matters in public or unsecured settings

- ✓ **Tips:**
- ✓ Follow company policies for handling sensitive information
- ✓ Use secure methods for data management
- ✓ Avoid discussing confidential matters in unsecured settings

8 Can You Provide an Example of When You Made a Mistake and How You Addressed It?

Interviewer Purpose: To explore how you handle errors and learn from them
Applicant's Answer: In a previous role, I miscalculated project timelines, which led to delays I immediately informed my team and stakeholders, recalculated the timelines, and developed a revised plan to get back on track I also implemented a new checklist system to prevent similar errors in the future

- ✓ **Tips:**
- ✓ Describe the mistake and the immediate actions taken
- ✓ Explain the corrective measures and improvements implemented
- ✓ Highlight the learning outcomes from the experience

9 How Do You Approach Ethical Dilemmas in the Workplace?

Interviewer Purpose: To assess your decision-making process in complex ethical situations
Applicant's Answer: I approach ethical dilemmas by evaluating the situation based on company policies and ethical standards I consider the potential impact on all stakeholders and seek guidance from trusted colleagues or mentors if needed My goal is to make decisions that align with both ethical principles and organizational values

- ✓ **Tips:**
- ✓ Evaluate based on policies and ethical standards
- ✓ Consider the impact on all stakeholders
- ✓ Seek guidance if needed to ensure aligned decisions

10 What Would You Do If Asked to Lie for a Manager or Colleague?

Interviewer Purpose: To understand how you handle pressure to compromise your values

Applicant's Answer: If asked to lie for a manager or colleague, I would respectfully refuse and explain my commitment to honesty and transparency I would express my concerns and suggest alternative solutions that adhere to ethical standards If the situation persists, I would consider reporting it to appropriate channels

- ✓ **Tips:**
- ✓ Firmly and respectfully refuse to compromise your values
- ✓ Propose alternative solutions that align with ethical standards
- ✓ Report the issue if it continues despite your efforts

Chapter-8

Handling challenges when an Interview is NOT Going Well

When an interview seems to be going off track or encountering setbacks, it's crucial to remain calm and employ strategies to steer it back on course Here's a breakdown of what setbacks are, and how to handle them effectively during an interview:

What is a Setback in an Interview?

A setback in an interview refers to any situation or moment where the conversation is not progressing as planned or desired This could be due to:

1. **Misunderstanding**: The interviewer may misinterpret your responses, or you may misunderstand the question
2. **Off-Topic Questions**: The interviewer might ask questions that are not relevant to the role or your qualifications
3. **Negative Impressions**: The interview may inadvertently highlight a negative aspect of your background
4. **Poor Communication**: You might struggle to articulate your thoughts clearly or confidently
5. **Technical Issues**: In virtual interviews, technical difficulties can disrupt the flow

Tips for Handling Setbacks During an Interview

1. **Stay Calm and Composed**: Maintain your composure even if the interview isn't going as planned Take a deep breath and don't let frustration show Your ability to stay calm demonstrates resilience and professionalism

2. **Clarify and Redirect**: : If a question is unclear or off-topic, politely ask for clarification You can also redirect the conversation by addressing the core competencies or skills relevant to the role For example, if asked about an unrelated past experience, link it back to how it has prepared you for the current position

   Example: "I'm not sure I fully understand the context of your question Could you please elaborate on what you're looking for? However, I'd like to highlight how my experience with [related skill] has prepared me for this role"

3. **Address Misunderstandings Professionally**: If you realize you've misunderstood a question or given a less-than-ideal answer, acknowledge it and correct yourself This shows self-awareness and the ability to adapt

   Example: "I see now that I may not have fully addressed your question about my leadership experience Let me clarify by providing an example where I successfully led a project team"

4. **Focus on Your Strengths**: Reiterate your key strengths and experiences that align with the job requirements Use examples that showcase your skills and how they're relevant to the role you're applying for

   Example: "While we've discussed various aspects, I want to emphasize that my expertise in [specific skill or experience] directly aligns with the core requirements of this role"

5. **Ask for a Moment to Collect Your Thoughts**: If you need a moment to gather your thoughts, it's perfectly acceptable to request it This can help you provide a more coherent and thoughtful response

   Example: "That's an interesting question May I take a moment to think about my response to ensure I provide a comprehensive answers.

6. **Reframe the Conversation**: If the conversation is veering off course, gently steer it back to relevant topics by mentioning how your skills and experiences relate to the role

   Example: "I'd like to shift our focus back to how my background in [relevant skill] can contribute to [specific aspect of the role or company]"

7. **Use Positive Language**: Maintain a positive attitude, even when discussing setbacks or challenges This shows that you are solution-oriented and resilient

   Example: "While the situation presented some challenges, it also provided valuable learning opportunities Here's how I approached and overcame the obstacles…"

8. **Express Enthusiasm and Interest**: Reaffirm your interest in the role and the company This helps to maintain a positive tone and redirect the interview toward your enthusiasm for the position

   Example: "Despite the challenges we've discussed, I am very excited about this opportunity because it aligns perfectly with my career goals and interests"

Handling setbacks during an interview requires a combination of calmness, clarity, and strategic redirection By addressing issues directly, emphasizing your strengths, and maintaining a positive attitude, you can effectively navigate the interview and leave a strong impression

Stage-3

AFTER INTERVIEW

Chapter -9
Salary Negotiation

Salary negotiations during job interviews play a crucial role in shaping both the candidate's and the employer's expectations, as they determine the value placed on the skills and experience brought to the table. For candidates, negotiating salary is not only about securing fair compensation but also about establishing their worth in the professional marketplace, which can impact their future earning potential. Effective salary negotiations demonstrate confidence and a clear understanding of one's value, which can leave a positive impression on the employer. For employers, these discussions provide insight into a candidate's priorities and their ability to advocate for themselves, which can be an important indicator of their overall fit within the organization.

Research Thoroughly: Understand the industry standards and market rates to justify your salary expectations
Communicate Clearly: Be transparent about your needs and expectations, and explain how your skills and experience align with the role
Be Flexible: Be open to discussing other benefits and adjustments if the salary offer is lower than expected

Questions

1. **Are you open to negotiating your salary?**

Interviewer Purpose: To gauge your flexibility and willingness to discuss compensation terms
Applicant's Answer: Yes, I am open to negotiating my salary I believe that discussing compensation is an essential part of the job offer process, and I am confident we can reach a mutually agreeable figure that reflects my skills and experience
Tips: First Be clear about your flexibility and secondly the importance of reaching a fair agreement

2. **How would you approach a situation where the offered salary is lower than what you expected?**

Interviewer Purpose: To understand your strategy for handling salary offers that do not meet your expectations
Applicant's Answer: If I receive an offer below my expectations, I would first express my appreciation for the opportunity and then present a well-researched counteroffer based on industry standards and my qualifications I would also be open to discussing other benefits that might compensate for the lower salary
Tips: Research and prepare a well-justified counteroffer; be open to negotiating other aspects of the compensation package

3. **How would you handle negotiating salary when you have multiple job offers?**

Interviewer Purpose: To determine how you leverage multiple offers in negotiations
Applicant's Answer: With multiple offers, I would use the highest offer as leverage to negotiate a better salary with my preferred employer I would present each offer respectfully, explaining why the preferred employer is my top choice but that I need a competitive offer to make a decision
Tips: Use multiple offers to your advantage, but be honest and respectful in your negotiations

4. **How do you deal with a counteroffer from your current employer?**

Interviewer Purpose: To assess your approach to handling counteroffers
Applicant's Answer: If presented with a counteroffer, I would carefully evaluate it in the context of my career goals and the reasons I was considering a change I would weigh the counteroffer against the new opportunity to ensure it aligns with my long-term objectives
Tips: Consider your career goals and the reasons behind your job search when evaluating a counteroffer

5. **How would you discuss salary with a potential employer if you are currently unemployed?**

Interviewer Purpose: To understand your approach to discussing compensation while unemployed
Applicant's Answer: While unemployed, I would focus on highlighting my skills, experience, and the value I can bring to the role I would present a salary range based on my research and the market value for similar positions
Tips: Emphasize your qualifications and market research to justify your salary expectations

6. **What is your approach to salary negotiations when transitioning into a new industry?**

Interviewer Purpose: To determine how you handle salary expectations when switching industries
Applicant's Answer: In a new industry, I would research salary benchmarks for the role and emphasize the transferable skills and experience I bring I would also be open to discussing how my unique background can add value to the new industry
Tips: Highlight transferable skills and research industry standards to support your salary expectations

7. **How would you manage salary negotiations if you are relocating for the job?**

Interviewer Purpose: To assess how you handle compensation adjustments related to relocation
Applicant's Answer: For relocation, I would consider the cost of living in the new area and adjust my salary expectations accordingly I would ensure the compensation reflects the increased living expenses and any other relocation-related costs
Tips: Factor in the cost of living and relocation expenses when negotiating your salary

8. **How do you handle salary negotiations when you have limited professional experience?**

Interviewer Purpose: To see how you negotiate compensation with limited experience
Applicant's Answer: With limited experience, I would focus on my potential, enthusiasm, and relevant skills or projects I would present a salary range that reflects my current level but also shows my eagerness to grow and contribute
Tips: Emphasize potential and enthusiasm, and be realistic about your salary expectations

9. **What is your approach to salary discussions if you are being promoted within your current company?**

Interviewer Purpose: To evaluate how you handle internal promotions and salary adjustments
Applicant's Answer: During an internal promotion, I would discuss how my new role and responsibilities justify a salary increase I would provide evidence of my contributions and how the new position aligns with my career progression
Tips: Highlight your increased responsibilities and contributions to justify the promotion salary

10. **How would you approach salary negotiations if you are re-entering the workforce after a career break?**

Interviewer Purpose: To understand how you address salary expectations after a career gap
Applicant's Answer: If re-entering the workforce, I would discuss how my skills have evolved during the break and how they apply to the role I would ensure my salary expectations align with current industry standards and reflect my refreshed expertise
Tips: Focus on the skills and experiences gained during your career break and their relevance to the role

Chapter -10
Reasons for Not Getting Offers After a Successful Interview

Securing a job interview often feels like a significant accomplishment, especially after preparing meticulously and delivering a strong performance However, it is not uncommon for candidates to find themselves in the unfortunate position of not receiving an offer despite what seemed like a successful interview Understanding the underlying reasons why this might occur can help candidates improve their chances in future opportunities This chapter delves into the various factors that may contribute to not receiving a job offer after an interview, even when the interview itself appeared to go well

1 **Cultural Fit Concerns**

One of the primary reasons for not receiving a job offer despite a successful interview is a mismatch in cultural fit Organizations often prioritize cultural compatibility as much as technical skills and qualifications Even if you excelled in answering questions and demonstrated your abilities, the hiring team may have concerns about whether you align with the company's values, work environment, and team dynamics For example, if the company places a high value on collaborative teamwork and you have emphasized your preference for independent work, this could be a red flag

Tip: During interviews, research the company's culture and values Tailor your responses to demonstrate how your personal values and work style align with the organization's culture

2 **Competitive Candidate Pool**

In highly competitive fields, even a strong interview performance may not guarantee an offer if other candidates are also exceptionally qualified The hiring team might find another candidate whose skills and experiences are slightly more aligned with the role or who better meets the specific needs of the position This is often the case in industries where numerous highly qualified individuals are vying for the same role

Tip: Highlight your unique strengths and experiences that set you apart from other candidates Demonstrate your value through specific examples and achievements

3 **Budgetary Constraints**

Sometimes, internal factors such as budgetary constraints can impact the hiring decision Even if you are the ideal candidate for the role, the company might face unforeseen budget cuts or financial issues that prevent them from extending an offer This situation is less about your performance and more about the company's financial situation

Tip: If you sense that budget issues might be a concern, inquire about the company's financial health and the stability of the position during your interview

4 **Hiring Manager's Preferences**

The final decision often rests with the hiring manager, whose personal preferences and biases can influence the outcome While you may have performed well in the interview, the hiring manager might have a particular vision or preference that sways their decision For instance, they might prefer a candidate with a specific type of experience or a different communication style

Tip: Try to build rapport with the hiring manager and understand their expectations Tailor your answers to address what you perceive as their key concerns and preferences

5 **Role or Job Description Changes**

The requirements for the role may evolve between the time of your interview and the final decision The company might adjust the job description, alter the responsibilities, or even change the role's focus based on emerging needs or organizational changes If your skill set no longer aligns with the updated role, this can impact the decision

Tip: During the interview, seek clarification on the role's key responsibilities and ask if there are any upcoming changes or challenges that might affect the role

6 **Reference and Background Checks**

Even if your interview performance was strong, issues arising from reference checks or background verification can impact the decision Negative feedback from references or discrepancies in your background check can lead to the withdrawal of an offer

Tip: Ensure your references are prepared and informed about the role you are applying for Address any potential concerns proactively during your interview

7 **Internal Candidate Preferences**

Companies often consider internal candidates for open positions as they are already familiar with the organization's culture and operations An internal candidate might be preferred over external candidates due to their existing relationship with the company, even if external candidates have strong credentials

Tip: If you are aware that the role might have internal candidates, emphasize your unique contributions and how you can bring a fresh perspective to the team

8 **Misalignment with Job Expectations**

There can be a misalignment between what you present as your capabilities and what the company expects from the role For instance, if your interview responses focused more on past achievements rather than how you would address specific challenges of the role, the hiring team might feel you are not fully aligned with the position's current needs

Tip: Ensure you understand the role's challenges and expectations thoroughly Tailor your responses to demonstrate how you would address these specific challenges effectively

Chapter -XI
Follow-Up Strategies Post-Interview

The interview process does not end when you walk out of the interview room Effective follow-up strategies can significantly influence the outcome of your job application Follow-up actions can reinforce your interest in the position, address any unanswered questions, and demonstrate professionalism and enthusiasm This chapter explores key follow-up strategies to employ after an interview to maximize your chances of success

1 **Send a Thank-You Email**

Purpose: A thank-you email expresses gratitude for the opportunity to interview and reinforces your interest in the position It also provides a chance to reiterate key points from the interview and address any additional thoughts or questions

- ✓ **Tips**:
- ✓ Send the thank-you email within 24 hours of the interview
- ✓ Personalize the message by referencing specific topics or conversations from the interview
- ✓ Keep the email concise and professional

Example: *"Dear [Interviewer's Name],*
Thank you for taking the time to discuss the [Position] role with me today I enjoyed learning more about [Company] and am enthusiastic about the opportunity to contribute to your team, especially in [specific area discussed] If you need any further information, please feel free to reach out

Best regards,
[Your Name]"

2 **Reiterate Your Interest**

Purpose: Reiterating your interest in the position reinforces your enthusiasm and commitment to the role It can be particularly effective if you feel the interview went well and you want to emphasize your eagerness

- ✓ **Tips**:
- ✓ Clearly state your continued interest in the role and company
- ✓ Mention specific aspects of the job or company that appeal to you
- ✓ Avoid being overly persistent or repetitive

Example: *"In addition to expressing my thanks, I want to reiterate how excited I am about the possibility of joining [Company] The discussion we had about [specific project or responsibility] aligns perfectly with my skills and interests, and I am keen to bring my experience to your team"*

3 **Address Unanswered Questions**

Purpose: If there were questions during the interview that you couldn't fully answer or if you think of additional information that could be valuable, a follow-up message is a good opportunity to provide this information

- ✓ **Tips**:
- ✓ Clearly reference the question or topic that was discussed
- ✓ Provide a thoughtful and concise answer or additional information
- ✓ Be sure to apologize for any confusion or incomplete responses

Example: *Dear [Interviewer's Name "During our interview, I realized that I didn't fully address the question about my experience with [specific skill] To clarify, [provide additional details or examples] I hope this additional information helps"*
Best regards,
[Your Name]"

4 **Follow-Up on Next Steps**

Purpose: Following up on next steps helps you stay informed about the status of your application and demonstrates your proactive attitude It's appropriate to send a follow-up email if you haven't received a response within the timeframe discussed during the interview

- ✓ **Tips**:
- ✓ Politely inquire about the status of your application and next steps in the hiring process
- ✓ Be respectful of the timeline provided during the interview
- ✓ Use a professional tone and avoid sounding impatient

Example: *"Dear [Interviewer's Name],*
I wanted to follow up regarding the [Position] role I'm very interested in the opportunity and would appreciate any updates you can provide on the next steps in the hiring process Thank you once again for considering my application
Best regards,
[Your Name]"

5 **Connect on Professional Networks**

Purpose: Connecting on professional networks such as LinkedIn can help you maintain contact with the interviewer and keep you on their radar It's a subtle way to show continued interest and professionalism

- ✓ **Tips**:
- ✓ Send a personalized connection request mentioning the interview
- ✓ Keep the connection request brief and professional
- ✓ Avoid making the connection request too soon after the interview

Example: *"Hi [Interviewer's Name],*
It was great meeting you during our interview for the [Position] role I'd love to connect with you on LinkedIn to stay updated on [Company] and any future opportunities
Best regards,
[Your Name]"

6 **Evaluate and Reflect**

Purpose: Post-interview reflection helps you evaluate your performance and identify areas for improvement It also prepares you for future interviews by analyzing what went well and what didn't
Tips:

- Reflect on your answers, body language, and the overall interaction
- Identify any areas where you could improve or adjust your approach
- Use this reflection to prepare for future interviews or follow-up discussions

Example: "*Reflecting on the interview, I realize that I could improve my response to questions about [specific topic] For future interviews, I will focus on providing more detailed examples and practicing my responses*"

7 **Send a Follow-Up Letter or Email**

Purpose: A formal follow-up letter or email can serve as a reiteration of your interest and gratitude It provides a more structured format for summarizing your key strengths and how they align with the role

- ✓ **Tips**:
- ✓ Use a formal tone and format
- ✓ Summarize your key qualifications and interest in the role
- ✓ Express appreciation for the opportunity to interview

Example: *"Dear [Interviewer's Name],*
Thank you for the opportunity to discuss the [Position] role at [Company] I am very enthusiastic about the chance to bring my [specific skills or experiences] to your team I am particularly excited about [specific project or aspect of the role] and believe my background in [relevant field] aligns well with your needs I look forward to the possibility of working together
Sincerely,
[Your Name]"

Effective follow-up strategies are crucial in reinforcing your candidacy and demonstrating your professionalism and interest in the role By sending thank-you notes, addressing any additional information, and inquiring about next steps, you can positively influence the hiring decision Remember to maintain a balance between persistence and professionalism to keep yourself in the best possible position for securing the job offer. fs

With you and for you

Dr Y Narasimha Raja

Ph.D., MBA, M.Sc. Psychology
Asst. Professor –School of Management,
Presidency University, Bengaluru

Email: ynraja.phd@gmail.com
Web: www.ynraja.com
Mob: +(91)8073205840

www.ingramcontent.com/pod-product-compliance
Lightning Source LLC
LaVergne TN
LVHW070843160826
845684LV00008B/62